SERIES EDITOR: LEE JOHNSON

OSPREY MILITARY MEN-AT-ARMS

SPANISH ARMY OF THE NAPOLEONIC WARS (1) 1793–1808

TEXT BY
RENÉ CHARTRAND

COLOUR PLATES BY
BILL YOUNGHUSBAND

First published in Great Britain in 1998 by Osprey Publishing
Elms Court, Chapel Way, Botley, Oxford OX2 9LP.

© 1998 Osprey Publishing Ltd.

All rights reserved. Apart from any fair dealing for the purpose of private study, research, criticism or review, as permitted under the Copyright, Designs and Patents Act, 1988, no part of this publication may be reproduced, stored in a retrieval system, or transmitted in any form or by any means, electronic, electrical, chemical, mechanical, optical, photocopying, recording or otherwise, without the prior permission of the copyright owner. Enquiries should be addressed to the Publishers.

ISBN 1 1 85532 763 5

Printed through World Print Ltd., Hong Kong

98 99 00 01 02   10 9 8 7 6 5 4 3 2 1

Editors: Sharon van der Merwe and Nikolai Bogdanovic
Design: Alan Hamp @ Design for Books

For a catalogue of all titles published by Osprey Military, Automotive and Aviation please write to:
The Marketing Manager, Osprey Publishing Ltd, PO Box 140, Wellingborough, Northants NN8 4ZA

TITLE PAGE **Spain's full coat-of-arms during the Napoleonic Wars depicted at the centre a blue oval with three golden lilies (the arms of the reigning Bourbon family), superimposed on the quartered arms of Castile and Leon, the medieval kingdoms, to which other realms, from Navarra to Granada, were later united and represented in the many outer coats-of-arms. A simpler basic design with only the arms of Castile and Leon with the Bourbon's central oval was often used. From the title page of an illustrated** *Estado Militar* **(Army Register) of 1789. (Anne S.K. Brown Military Collection, Brown University, Providence. Ph: R. Chartrand)**

Author's note

This volume is the first of three that will examine the organisation, uniforms and weapons of the Spanish army in Europe during the Napoleonic wars, as well as providing a glimpse of its sea-soldiers. This first part deals with the period starting in 1793 with the forces that fought the French, later the British and Portuguese and, by 1808, were again fighting the French armies of Napoleon. The second part will cover the varied forces that gave such desperate and stubborn resistance during 1808–1812. The third part will examine the reorganisation of the Spanish army, undertaken with massive British assistance in the final years of the great struggle against Napoleon's empire. Based on Spanish sources as well as newly discovered British documents, it is hoped this study will form the most extensive source yet published in English on the material culture of the Spanish peninsular forces between 1793 and 1815.

The names of Spanish personalities are given in their original Spanish form. Thus King Ferdinand VII is Fernando VII.

Colour hues of Spanish uniforms generally followed practices in other European armies. Thus, blue meant a very dark blue; similarly, green was very dark, but emerald green was a medium green. Scarlet was indifferently red or scarlet, but crimson was more reddish than its British counterpart.

Publishers' note

Readers may wish to study this title in conjunction with some of the many titles in the Men-at-Arms series covering the Napoleonic period in addition to the following Osprey publications:

MAA 87 *Napoleon's Marshals*
MAA 68 *Napoleon's Line Chasseurs*
MAA 84 *Wellington's Generals*
MAA 96 *Artillery Equipment of the Napoleonic Wars*
MAA 114 *Wellington's Infantry (1)*
MAA 119 *Wellington's Infantry (2)*
MAA 130 *Wellington's Heavy Cavalry*
MAA 141 *Napoleon's Line Infantry*
MAA 146 *Napoleon's Light Infantry*
Campaign 48 *Salamanca 1812*
Campaign 59 *Vittoria 1813*

Artist's note

Readers may care to note that the original paintings from which the colour plates in this book were prepared are available for private sale. All reproduction copyright whatsoever is retained by the Publisher. All enquiries should be addressed to:

Bill Younghusband
Moorfield, Kilcolman West, Buttevant, Co. Cork, Eire.

The Publishers regret that they can enter into no correspondence upon this matter.

SPANISH ARMY OF THE NAPOLEONIC WARS (1) 1793–1808

INTRODUCTION

During the reign of King Carlos III (1759–1788), Spain enjoyed a revival as a major European power. There was a considerable influx of ideas in all fields, especially from France and Italy, while educated Spaniards made grand tours across Europe seeking new notions. Arts, sciences and the economy flourished. Although a deeply religious and staunchly Roman Catholic society, Spain was one of the first countries to ban the Jesuit Order which stood accused of too much political meddling. This period became known as the *Ilustracion* – the 'Age of Enlightenment' in Spain.

Since the reign of Fernando and Isabella (1469–1516) the Spanish realm had been a union of five kingdoms. But the country's natural geography and poor roads made communication difficult. Thus, the 12 million people in Spain identified strongly with their native areas. A large proportion of the populace, about 600,000, were *hidalgos* of noble blood, a few being the powerful and wealthy 'Grandees', but most were poor though fiercely proud. The many church orders and monasteries accounted for another 200,000 persons. The rest were *El Comun*, the common people. Thus, while the country increasingly opened to various influences and ideas, its values remained strongly influenced by traditional regional and national considerations.

The army was transformed during the 18th century by an influx of progressive officers who modernised and expanded it. It was closely modelled on the French armies of Louis XIV and Louis XV in tactical doctrine, organisation, armament and uniforms. Following the Seven Years' War, Prussian-style drill and discipline were introduced, but were resisted more strongly than in other armies by the proud and individualistic Spanish soldiers. Attempts to apply corporal punishment, for example, often met with violent and even bloody reactions by the men. And they had the sympathy of many of their equally proud officers. So, while discipline was certainly not the same as in Prussia, Spanish regiments were nevertheless well behaved, filled with generally good-humoured men toughened by the hardships of a soldier's life. In battle, they were often brave to the point of carelessness, and were thus sometimes difficult to control. The army also had several Swiss and Walloon regiments, less given to all-out attacks, but renowned for their steadiness under fire. The reforms in the army had given

Manuel Godoy protected by troopers of the Life Guards from an angry mob. Encouraged by Prince Fernando, the mob sacked and burned Godoy's palace at Aranjuez on 18 March 1808. Godoy, who had schemed to take the Spanish throne for himself, instantly lost all powers and King Carlos IV abdicated in favour of Fernando.
(Print after Myrbach)

In early May 1808, during a stormy meeting at Bayonne, where the Spanish royal family had been summoned by Napoleon, an angry Carlos IV forced his son Fernando VII to abdicate in turn. Napoleon then sent both to a golden retreat and named his brother Joseph as Joseph-Napoleon, King of Spain and of the Indies. (Print after Myrbach)

The surrender of General Dupont's French army to the Spanish forces at Bailen in July 1808 was to have extraordinary consequences throughout Europe. Until then, the French imperial army had seemed invincible, but now for the first time, a large French corps which included units of the Imperial Guard, was beaten by a Spanish army. This victory gave hope to all in Europe who resisted Napoleon's rule. (Print after Maurice Orange)

generally favourable results during the American War of Independence. It was a confident, well-trained but small army (about 78,000 men) that Carlos III, one of Europe's benevolent 'enlightened despots', passed on to his son in 1788.

Carlos IV, who reigned from 1788 to 1808, was a kindly, dim-witted man, utterly unsuited to rule, and certainly not enlightened. Fond of hunting almost daily when not tinkering with clock mechanisms, he showed little interest in anything else, including the affairs of state. The vacuum in power was soon assumed by Queen Maria Luisa's handsome young lover, Manuel Godoy, a skilful but unscrupulous rogue who became the most powerful man in Spain. Godoy had started his career as a trooper in the Life Guards and progressed from the queen's bed to become, in effect, the prime minister. Somehow he also obtained the confidence and trust of the king, an extraordinary feat, given the nature of his relationship with the queen.

During the early 1790s, Godoy consolidated his position of power, filling the court with his supporters, and exiling or jailing anyone whom he considered threatened his influence at court. With Godoy at the helm, diverting royal revenues to his own coffers, the *Ilustracion* in Spain was indeed over.

The events of the French Revolution worried Spain. The 'Nootka Crisis' of 1790 brought Spain to the brink of war with Great Britain over territorial claims on the coast of present-day British Columbia (Canada) where there was already a Spanish fort. When the French National Assembly refused to respect the alliance, Spain settled as best it could and was left to find a new diplomatic equation. It was not long in coming. The Spanish royal family were close relations of the unfortunate French king, and with the influx of French noble émigrés, royalist Spain soon found itself in direct opposition to republican France. The French revolutionaries twice rejected offers of neutrality and safe conduct for the French royal family, then went further and declared war on Spain on 7 March 1793, proclaiming that 'the victors of Jemmapes would again find the strength to exterminate all the kings in Europe, which made them win previously'.

Things did not go according to French plans and in the summer of 1793 one Spanish army successfully held the western Pyrenees, while another, under General Ricardos, an officer with an excellent reputation, invaded Roussillon and western Provence. But Ricardos fell ill and died in early 1794, as did his successor, General O'Reilly, a skilled Irish officer. The Spanish army suddenly found itself without its two best commanders. Another Spanish corps assisted the British, Neapolitan and Piedmontese in the occupation of the great French Mediterranean naval base at Toulon until its evacuation in December 1793.

In 1794, the French armies counter-attacked in overwhelming numbers, and the Spanish retreated while fighting several fierce engagements. At Black Mountain (17–20 November), both the French commander Dugommier and the Spanish general La Union were killed. But with the French now invading northern Spain, a peace treaty was signed on 22 July 1795 at Basel. In exchange for the relatively unimportant colony of Santo Domingo (now the Dominican Republic), Godoy negotiated the withdrawal of the French and was thus proclaimed the 'Prince of Peace' by Carlos IV.

But peace did not last very long. Spain found itself allied with France in August 1796 by the Treaty of San Ildefonso and at war with its old enemy, Great Britain. The British launched several large-scale naval raids against Spanish ports in Europe and overseas during 1797. The peninsular army now stood at 150,000 men. In the West Indies, Trinidad was taken, but the British were beaten off at San Juan, Puerto Rico. A British fleet appeared at Cadiz on 5 July and proceeded to blockade and bombard the city. But Admiral Mazarredo had already organised its defences for such an attack. The Spanish garrison and naval forces put up such a spirited resistance that the fleet went away two days later. Another British fleet, under Horatio Nelson, attacked Santa Cruz de Tenerife in the Canary Islands in July. On 22 July, a first landing was repulsed with losses, but Nelson tried again in the early morning of the 24th. Spanish gunfire devastated the British landing party led by Nelson, who lost his right arm to a cannonball. Another British landing party found itself surrounded by Spanish regulars and militias in one of the churches of Santa Cruz and surrendered.

In November 1798, however, the British attacked the island of Menorca which they captured without much difficulty.

In 1801, the last major campaign of the war was directed against Britain's old ally, Portugal. Napoleon Bonaparte wished to isolate Portugal and convinced Godoy and Carlos IV to invade with the aid of a French corps. As the 'Prince of Peace' set up his HQ in an orange grove near the Portuguese border at Badajos, wags in Madrid soon baptised the whole operation the 'War of the Oranges'. The campaign got under way in May, and Portugal, overwhelmed by three armies numbering some 60,000 men, sued for peace which was signed on 6 June. It had to concede its province of Olivença to Spain and close its ports to British ships.

After the short interlude of peace brought by the Treaty of Amiens in 1802–1803, Spain was once again at war with Great Britain as the uncomfortable ally of Napoleon, now emperor of the French. The still-powerful Spanish fleet under Admiral Gravina was subordinated to Admiral Villeneuve's French fleet. The great British naval victory at Trafalgar on 21 October 1805 was a disastrous defeat for Spain signalling its demise as a naval power.

The following year a British expedition captured Buenos Aires and Montevideo in what is now Argentina and Uruguay, but the British troops left in the garrison were overwhelmed by the local colonial volunteers and regulars. Another British force captured Montevideo in January 1807, but was defeated at Buenos Aires and evacuated the area in February.

In 1807, Napoleon called on Spain to help him impose his continental blockade more vigorously by providing an army corps of 14,000

A fusilier of the 2nd Regiment of Voluntarios de Cataluña, 1789. This light infantry unit recruited from mountaineers wore a mixture of uniform and local costume: an ample blue coat (gambeto), cuff flaps and breeches, yellow cuffs, lining and waistcoat, pewter buttons, white hat lace. (Anne S.K. Brown Military Collection, Brown University, Providence. Ph: R. Chartrand)

Royal Corps of Artillery gunner, 1789. He wears a blue coat and breeches, with scarlet collar, cuffs, and waistcoat, gold lace edging the collar, brass buttons, and a bicorn laced yellow. Until 1802 the uniform of the artillery remained basically unchanged. The gun carriage is painted red. (Anne S.K. Brown Military Collection, Brown University, Providence. Ph: R. Chartrand)

Fijo de Puerto Rico Regiment fusilier, c. 1790–1800. This colonial unit was the only regular infantry of the garrison of San Juan which repulsed the British attack on the city in 1797. It later saw action against the French at the 1809 siege of the city of Santo Domingo (Dominican Republic) with the now allied British troops of Sir George Prevost. The uniform of the Puerto Rico Regiment was a white coat with blue collar, cuffs and lapels (with only three buttons each), white metal buttons, white waistcoat and breeches, and a plain bicorn hat. The regiment was sent to Venezuela in 1815 and absorbed into the Granada and Leon infantry regiments in 1816. After a plate by Jose Campeche. (Archivo General de Simancas)

men to patrol the coasts of Denmark, as well as providing passage for a French army sent to invade Portugal. Godoy acquiesced, and the Marquis de la Romana was soon in Denmark with his corps. Meanwhile, Marshal Junot marched through Spain with a French army of 20,000 men. He was joined by a small and somewhat reluctant Spanish force. Junot then invaded Portugal, easily sweeping aside all resistance, and entered Lisbon on 27 November.

Napoleon wanted to consolidate his grip on the whole peninsula and hinted that he might establish separate kingdoms for Godoy and others. There was thus a huge power game going on in the palace corridors. The ordinary people of Spain, utterly discontented with the politics and abuses of Manuel Godoy, revolted at Arranuez, on the night of 17 March 1808. A huge crowd took to the streets and stormed and ransacked Godoy's palace; he barely escaped with his life, his power being instantly broken. Following the riot which deposed Godoy, Carlos IV reluctantly abdicated in favour of his son Fernando, with whom he was feuding. Napoleon now played his hand and convened the Spanish royal family to Bayonne to arbitrate matters. On 6 June, under pressure from all sides and following a stormy meeting with his parents, Fernando also abdicated, leaving Napoleon to proclaim his brother Joseph as King of Spain.

But the Spanish people would not accept a French puppet king and resented the French 'allied' army of 80,000 men under Marshal Murat that was already in Spain. On 2 May, the populace of Madrid rose in revolt, killing some 500 French troops before being bloodily put down by cavalry charges and firing squads. News of this unexpected uprising spread like wildfire and was the signal for a general revolt.

During his long 'reign', Manuel Godoy had inflicted severe damage on what had been excellent military forces. Even before the British naval victory at St. Vincent in 1796, Admiral Mazarredo had written to warn Godoy of the dangers to Spain of naval decline. Unfortunately the neglect of both the army and the navy became especially severe following the War of the Oranges. For the navy, the reckoning came at Trafalgar in 1805. In the army, regiments were increasingly short of men and supplies. When Romana's Corps was assembled to march north, men and horses were drafted from other regiments to bring the corps up to strength.

Perhaps even worse, the cavalry and infantry regimental officers, two-thirds of whom were *hidalgos* with the rest coming up from the ranks, had not kept up with advances in military science. For most officers, theoretical training was almost non-existent.

Only the artillery and the engineers had academies. Engineer officers instructed a few infantry and cavalry officers and cadets at Zamora and Barcelona, but this was the exception.

In the spring and summer of 1808, however, the armed forces, such as they were, took up arms against the world's best army, while new units spontaneously sprang up all over Spain. Corps and armies were somehow rapidly organised, commanders appointed and soon, tens of thousands were marching against the French. One of these new corps, numbering over 21,000 men under General Castaños, was in Andalucia when on 19 July it intercepted at Bailen a French army of the same strength under General Dupont. Outfought and outmanoeuvred, a stunned world soon learned that Dupont's whole force had surrendered to a Spanish army!

For the first time since Napoleon's rise to power, a large corps of his invincible French imperial army had been not only beaten, but entirely lost. This incredible news gave hope to all in Europe who were struggling against Napoleon's domination.

ORGANISATION AND UNIFORMS

The Spanish army was organised much like other western European armies of the later 18th century, and was modelled mainly on the French army. There was a general staff led by 'captains-general', a rank equivalent of field marshal, and a sizeable administrative body of staff officers, intendants and auditors.

The infantry and cavalry regiments of the army were divided into the Royal Guard and the line. These were mostly recruited from native Spaniards, but there were foreign regiments, the most important being the Swiss contingents which amounted to about 13,000 men. The regulars were assisted by battalions of provincial and urban militia. Then followed the specialist corps such as the artillery, the engineers and other auxiliary corps. Outlying areas such as Ceuta in Morocco or the Canary Islands also had their own troops. In 1808, the army numbered about 7,000 officers and 130,000 NCOs and enlisted men, including 30,000 mobilised militiamen.

Spanish soldiers dressed in uniforms that were generally similar in styles to other European armies. The clothing was generally of good quality but the coat and waistcoat had to last for about 30 months, a shirt and a pair of breeches 15 months. This is why Spanish soldiers were seen in Germany and Denmark in 1807 with older style uniforms.[1]

Undress or 'fatigue' dress consisted of a round jacket and breeches or pantaloons the same colour as the regular waistcoat and breeches.

The Duke of Osuna with his family, 1790. The duke was colonel of the regiment of Spanish Guards Infantry and a progressive officer much interested in tactical innovations. For instance he felt, rightly as Napoleon was to prove, that close artillery support could enhance battlefield success. He did manage to introduce light artillery companies in the Guards, but these innovations were swept away after a decade. In this painting, the duke wears an all-blue undress uniform with red collar and cuffs, silver embroidered lace and buttons, and silver-laced hat with a large red cockade. (Print after Goya)

---

[1] We do not find comprehensive information on clothing issues of all units for the period under study. However, in 1828, a coat was to last 45 months, a jacket 53 months, a greatcoat 4 years, a bearskin cap 6 years.

The jacket could have the collar and/or the cuffs of the facing colour. The sleeves were often attached to the jacket's shoulders by facing colour cords. Sandals with ribbon ties were often worn. The most common type of forage cap had a long pointed crown of the coat colour piped in the facing colour and facing colour turnup. Some cavalry also had a high-fronted cap.

Regimental rank badges in the Spanish forces were as follows: colonels had three laces on each cuff, lieutenant-colonels had two, majors had one; captains had epaulettes on each shoulder, lieutenants one on the right, second lieutenants (or ensigns) one on the left, and cadets wore an aiguillette. The officers' lace and epaulettes were of gold or silver, according to the button colour of the corps. While on duty, they wore a gilt gorget complete with a silver badge bearing the royal arms in at the centre.

Sergeants had epaulettes of the colour of the facing, corporals a white or yellow cloth lace edging the collar and cuffs. From 4 June 1807, one to four laces in the corps' facing colour worn on the upper sleeve could be awarded for long service by NCOs and enlisted men.

Since 1760, drummers in the Spanish forces had generally worn the livery of their Bourbon kings. This consisted of a blue coat or coatee faced with scarlet collar, cuff and turnbacks. If the unit had lapels, its drummers would have them in scarlet. The collar, cuffs and lapels were edged with the royal livery lace; a white chain on a crimson or red ground. The buttons were those of the regiment. Infantry drum-majors wore the same blue faced red with the livery lace but added many rich features such as silver or gold lace, wide scarlet baldric with elaborate embroidery, lace and fringes, multi-coloured plumes on the bicorn and silver-trimmed long cane. Brass drums with blue hoops were usual at the time of the Napoleonic Wars, but the older style wooden drums painted blue with the royal arms in front were still in use. The drum-belt was white with brass drum stick holders.

There were a few exceptions to this rule: in foot troops such as the regiments belonging to the queen (*Reina*), the regiment of sappers and miners who had red coats, and the foreign regi-ments who wore their colonels' liveries.

In mounted units, the rules regarding the royal livery were apparently much more relaxed for trumpeters and kettle-drummers. From the end of the 18th century, trumpeters of the line cavalry regiments in the peninsula had reversed colours with the lining or turnbacks of the uniform coat. For example, a trumpeter of the Villaviciosa Dragoons is shown in a red hussar dress, and another of the Infante Cavalry wears red faced with yellow in 1807. However, royal regiments such as Rey had the king's livery and the queen's regiments wore her red livery lined with blue.

Bandsmen in Spanish infantry regiments appear to have worn scarlet coats. For instance,

Army surgeon Joseph Montegut, c. 1800. Montegut was the senior surgeon of Spanish forces in Louisiana, a Spanish colony until 1803. He wears the medical corps uniform: blue coat and breeches, scarlet collar, cuffs and waistcoat, silver lace and buttons. Detail from a family painting by Jose Salazar. (Louisiana State Museum, New Orleans)

Light Artillery Brigade of the king's Guardia de Corps (Life Guard), gunner, 1801. This unit had 65 men uniformed in blue coatees, with lapels, cuff flaps and breeches, scarlet collars, cuffs, turnbacks and waistcoat, white lace edging lapels, pewter buttons, black short boots, round hats with bearskin crests, white bands and red tufts, and blue housings edged white. (Anne S.K. Brown Military Collection, Brown University, Providence. Ph: R. Chartrand)

LEFT **Guardias Españolas Regiment, 1801.** The centre figure is a grenadier wearing a bearskin cap, on the left is a light infantryman wearing a round hat, on the right is a fusilier wearing a bicorn. The uniform is a blue coat and breeches, red collar, cuffs, lapels, turnbacks and waistcoat, pewter buttons, white lace. (Anne S.K. Brown Military Collection, Brown University, Providnece. Ph: R. Chartrand)

Suhr shows Zamora Regiment musicians in scarlet coats with black facings edged white, and Princesa Regiment musicians wearing the same colours, but in the hussar style with black bearskin busbies.

With regard to hairstyles, powdered hair and queues were abolished from 1793 and the men were clean shaven until moustaches and sideburns became increasingly fashionable from the early 1800s.

Generals and Staff Officers

The Spanish armies had about 400 general officers of various grades before 1808. The most senior rank, after King Carlos IV and Manuel Godoy, the 'Generalissimo' who was also Admiral and 'Prince of Peace', was that of the five captain-generals. The hundreds of others did not all hold active commands with the army. Many were town governors in Spain or held a senior post in the colonies, others served some more-or-less important staff function, and some were simply retired from duty but could be recalled to the active list.

The full dress or full gala uniform of captain-generals was a blue coat, with scarlet collar, cuffs, lapels and turnbacks, gold buttons, gold embroidery at the seams and edging the facings, two additional gold embroidered laces on each cuff (thus making three laces), a scarlet waistcoat edged with gold embroidery, a scarlet sash with three rows of gold embroidery, scarlet breeches, a bicorn laced gold, edged with a white plume border and a red standing plume, and high black boots. The dress or gala uniform was the same colours but without embroidery at the seams. The 'small' uniform for ordinary duties was a coat of the same colours, but with gold embroidery edging only the lapels and cuffs, and a buff waistcoat and breeches.

Lieutenant-generals wore the same as a captain-general but without embroidery at the seams and with two rows of embroidery at the cuffs and sash, a bicorn laced gold edged with a black plume border and a red standing plume.

Mariscales de Campo (roughly, a major-general) wore the same as a lieutenant-general, but with only one row of embroidered lace on the cuffs and sash, and a bicorn laced gold and edged only with a red standing plume.

Brigadier-generals had a blue coat, with scarlet collar, cuffs, lapels and turnbacks, silver buttons, silver embroidered lace edging the facings, a scarlet waistcoat and breeches, and a silver laced hat. The ordinary uniform was the same, with silver lace edging only the cuffs and lapels, and a white waistcoat and breeches.

The *Ayudante de Campo* (camp adjutant) wore a blue coat, with scarlet collar, cuffs, lapels and turnbacks, gold buttons, gold lace edging the facings, a scarlet waistcoat edged with gold lace, and blue pantaloons.

Often, generals were also colonels of a regiment, and many preferred to wear their regimental uniform with their rank shown on the cuffs; three laces for colonel and one or more embroidered laces above for the general's rank. This is shown in the portraits of many generals.

RIGHT **Rey Regiment grenadier, 1801**, wearing a white coatee, with violet cuffs and lapels, scarlet collar and piping, brass buttons stamped with '*Rey*', yellow laces at the cuffs and a bearskin cap. Note the long moustaches, also a distinction of grenadiers. The coatee is of the new cut, introduced generally from 1802, with lapels squared and closed to the waist. (Anne S.K. Brown Military Collection, Brown University, Providence. Ph: R. Chartrand)

FAR RIGHT **Africa Regiment, fusilier, 1801.** This regiment distinguished itself against the French during the Roussillon campaign in 1795, earning the right to wear a distinctive oval sleeve badge, not shown on this plate. In 1798 it was sent to Puerto Rico to reinforce the garrison following the repulse of the British attack on San Juan and went back to the Peninsula in late 1799. The uniform consisted of white coatees and collar, black cuffs, lapels and piping, and brass buttons. (Anne S.K. Brown Military Collection, Brown University, Providence. Ph: R. Chartrand)

Administrative and Staff Officers

The Spanish army had an elaborate corps of about 350 administrative officers. Nearly all served in Spain, with a few posted in Havana. They controlled finances and pay and various aspects in the procurement and making of supplies, food and lodgings. Generals and governors, the 'officers of the sword', could not by-pass the 'officers of the quill pen', the army intendants, commissaries and senior accountants when planning operations.

Administrative officers wore a blue single-breasted long coat (without turnbacks) with a scarlet collar, cuffs, lining and waistcoat, white stockings, silver buttons, a plain bicorn hat with a silver cockade loop, and blue breeches. The various grades had a complicated system of silver embroidered lace on the coat. Army intendants, for instance, had rich broad silver embroidery, resembling that of generals, edging the collar, coat front, pocket flaps and waistcoat, the cuffs having two rows of lace denoting their senior rank. Provincial intendants had one row. *Comisario de Guerra* (army commissaries), provincial treasurers and senior auditors had elaborate buttonhole embroidery set in various ways. These senior officers carried long canes with gold pommels for intendants, silver for commissaries. Lower grades such as writing clerks had blue cuffs with silver double lilies and silver embroidered lace at the collar. Army auditors had a distinct uniform, consisting of a blue coat, violet collar and cuffs, scarlet turnbacks, gold lace edging the collar, cuffs and pocket flaps, gold buttons, no epaulettes, and a white or buff waistcoat and breeches. All administrative officers carried swords, but none had sashes, a distinction reserved for senior 'officers of the sword'.

ABOVE **Fusilier, Voluntarios de Castilla Regiment, 1801,** wearing a white coatee, with crimson cuffs, lapels, collar and piping, pewter buttons. This print shows white lace on the lapels, an ornament very rarely used in the line infantry. (Anne S.K. Brown Military Collection, Brown University, Providence. Ph: R. Chartrand)

ABOVE RIGHT **Fusilier, Hibernia (Irish) Regiment, 1801,** wearing a white coatee, with scarlet lapels and cuffs, green collar and piping, pewter buttons. Between 1791 and 1805, the Irish regiments, which previously had distinctive uniforms, wore the same coat colours as the rest of the Spanish infantry. (Anne S.K. Brown Military Collection, Brown University, Providence. Ph: R. Chartrand)

Staff officers in towns and cities were generally responsible for municipal upkeep and order, and for providing various facilities for regiments arriving and leaving. Governors of towns had blue coats and breeches with scarlet cuffs and waistcoats, and gold lace edging the coat and waistcoat. A *Teniente del Rey* ('king's lieutenant', or lieutenant-governor) and a *Mayor de Plaza* (a town major) had gold buttonholes. Other officers attached to a garrison staff wore an all-blue uniform, consisting of a single-breasted coat with a gold lily at the collar, gold buttons and their rank badges (i.e. two gold laces on the cuffs for a lieutenant-colonel), and also a bicorn edged with gold. There was a *Maestro Mayor de Obras* too (basically a superintendent of works to maintain the town's fortifications) who wore a blue coat and breeches, red plain cuffs (no buttons), lining and piping edging the pocket flaps, a yellow collar, silver buttons, and narrow silver lace edging the waistcoat.

THE ROYAL GUARD

The troops of the royal household originated in the early 18th century, having been organised shortly after Felipe V, the grandson of France's Louis XIV, ascended the Spanish throne. It bore a strong resemblance to the French royal guards – even the uniforms were of the same blue-faced-red livery of the French Bourbon family. Except for the Guard Halberdiers, the units were detached in the field and amounted to some 6,000 men. In 1808 most of the guards joined the fight against the French. For instance, following the Madrid uprising on 2 May, the Life Guards simply left the Escurial with their standards and joined the patriotic forces. The guard units were as follows.

Guardias de Corps

The Life Guards (raised 1704) consisted of four cavalry companies, the 1st Spanish, the 2nd Italian, the 3rd Flemish and the 4th American (raised 27 January 1795), each of 225 officers and troopers including two trumpeters and a kettle-drummer. They were reduced to three companies of 180 men in 1803 following the disbandment of the Flemish

2nd Regiment of Voluntarios de Cataluña, fusilier, 1801 in a blue coatee with yellow collar, cuffs, lapels and turnbacks, a light grey ample coat with yellow cuffs slung over the shoulder, pewter buttons, white waistcoat and breeches, plain hat, and buff belly cartridge box. (Anne S.K. Brown Military Collection, Brown University, Providence. Ph: R. Chartrand)

Ruttiman (Swiss) Regiment fusilier, 1801, in a blue coat, with scarlet collar, cuffs, lapels, shoulder straps and turnbacks, blue cuff flaps and hearts on turnbacks, white piping, pewter buttons, white waistcoat and breeches. (Anne S.K. Brown Military Collection, Brown University, Providence. Ph: R. Chartrand)

company. From 1797 to 1803, there was also a *Brigada de Artilleria Volante* of 67 officers and light artillerymen with eight light cannon in the Life Guards. Officers of the Life Guards ranked as colonels in the line cavalry, NCOs ranked as captains and lieutenants, and troopers as ensigns or gentlemen cadets.

Uniforms consisted of a blue coat and breeches, with scarlet collar, cuffs, lapels, turnbacks and waistcoat, silver buttons, silver lace edging the collar, cuffs and lapels, silver epaulettes, silver lace edging the waistcoat, and a hat laced silver.[2] Each company had a silver laced bandoleer of the company colour; scarlet for the first, green for the second, yellow for the third and violet for the fourth.

The 1797 uniform of the light artillery is illustrated elsewhere in this book. From *c.* 1802 it was the same as the Life Guards, but the lapels were pointed rather than squared: they wore a black Tarleton helmet with a black fur crest, silver fittings and a red plume, tight blue pantaloons with white lace, and no bandoleers.

Guardias Alabarderos

The Guard of Halberdiers Company (formed 1707) was a palace guard unit of four officers and 100 men (later 150) armed with halberds. It was recruited from veterans in the Guard and in the rest of the army.

Uniforms were a blue coat and breeches, with a scarlet collar, cuffs, turnbacks and waistcoat, silver buttons, silver buttonhole lace on lapels set in 1-2-3 from the top, silver knee garters, silver lace edging the waistcoat, a hat laced silver, and red stockings for the men, and white for officers. It changed in about 1800, to scarlet lapels with silver buttonhole lace, and silver lace edging the collar and cuffs.

---

[2] On 8 March 1808, Life Guards retired from the service were instructed to wear the regimental uniform but with blue cuffs and a silver lion at the collar.

LEFT **Granaderos Voluntarios de Estado Regiment grenadier, 1801. The uniform was a blue coat, with buff lapels, cuffs and turnbacks, blue collar with a scarlet patch piped white, scarlet piping, white lace at the cuffs, pewter buttons, a white waistcoat edged with red piping, white breeches, a bearskin cap, and white accoutrements with a brass match case. (Anne S.K. Brown Military Collection, Brown University, Providence. Ph: R. Chartrand)**

Chasseur, Voluntarios de la Corona, 1801, wearing a blue dolman and long breeches, with scarlet collar, cuffs, cuff and pocket flaps, white cords and lace, pewter buttons, a white waistcoat with three rows of buttons, a round hat with a bearskin crest and a red plume, short black gaiters, a buff belly cartridge box and short sabre. (Anne S.K. Brown Military Collection, Brown University, Providence. Ph: R. Chartrand)

Guardias de Infanteria Espanola

The Spanish Guards Infantry Regiment was raised in 1704. The original four battalions were raised to six in 1791, each having seven companies of 100 men each, including one of grenadiers. The *Cazadores Artilleros* (Chasseurs-Artillerymen) of the Spanish Guard Infantry, raised 1793, had six companies, one for each battalion, of 105 officers and men, but were disbanded in 1803. Considerable reductions were made in 1803, when three battalions were disbanded, the number of fusiliers in the remaining three battalions was reduced to 50 per company, and the grenadier companies were limited to 100 men.

Uniforms were a blue coat and breeches, scarlet collar, cuffs, turnbacks and waistcoat, pewter buttons, white pointed buttonhole lace set in threes, white lace edging the waistcoat, and a hat edged white. Some sources show white lace edging the cuffs. In 1800 the collar changed to blue, and scarlet lapels were added to the coat, the lapels having white pointed buttonhole lace set in pairs, and white piping edging the facings. NCOs did not have buttonhole lace from 1800 but had narrow silver lace edging the collar and cuffs. Officers did not have buttonhole lace, but their collar, cuffs and lapels (from 1800) were edged with wide silver lace. NCOs and officers had also their regular rank badges.

The uniform of the Chasseurs-Artillerymen from 1793 was a blue coat and breeches, with scarlet cuffs, collar turnbacks and waistcoat, pewter buttons, white pointed buttonhole lace set in threes, no lace on the waistcoat, a round hat with brim turned up on the left side, a red plume, and white hat band. From 1800 the blue collar was piped scarlet, scarlet lapels were added with two pairs of white pointed buttonhole lace and one lace at the top of the lapel, and white lace edged the top of the cuffs. The white hat plumes were tipped with the company colour; red (1st company), sky blue (2nd), all white (3rd), yellow (4th), violet (5th) and green (6th).

Guardias de Infanteria Walonna

The Walloon Guards Infantry Regiment (raised 1704) had the same organisation and strength as the Spanish Guards Infantry Regiment. The Walloon Guards did not have companies of Chasseurs-Artillerymen. The uniform was the same as the Spanish Guards Infantry, but in the early 1790s the buttonhole lace was apparently set in pairs.

Carabineros Reales

The Royal Carabiniers (raised 1730) had four squadrons from 1793, each squadron having 276 men divided into four companies. There were six squadrons from 1802 when the two light cavalry squadrons (raised in 1800) serving as guards to the 'Prince of Peace' and Grand Admiral, Manuel Godoy, were added to the *Carabineros*.

The line squadrons wore a blue coat, cuffs and breeches, scarlet collar, lapels, turnbacks and waistcoat, white lace edging the cuffs and collar, pewter buttons, a hat laced white, and blue housings laced white.

Godoy's guards, generally called *Guardia del Almirante* (Admiral's Guard), consisted of a squadron of hussars and a squadron of mounted chasseurs. From 1800 to 1805, the hussar dress consisted of a blue dolman and tight pantaloons, scarlet collar, cuffs and pelisse edged with

BELOW, LEFT **Trooper, Infante Cavalry Regiment, 1801,** dressed in a blue coat, with white collar and lapels, violet cuffs, scarlet turnbacks and piping, pewter buttons, buff waistcoat and breeches, white hat lace, and red housings edged with white. (Anne S.K. Brown Military Collection, Brown University, Providence. Ph: R. Chartrand)

BELOW, RIGHT **Almansa Dragoon Regiment, trooper, 1801,** in a green coat, scarlet collar, turnbacks and piping, sky blue lapels, cuffs and turnbacks, triangle ornaments, pewter buttons, buff waistcoat and breeches, white hat lace, and green housings edged white. (Anne S.K. Brown Military Collection, Brown University, Providence. Ph: R. Chartrand)

white fur, pewter buttons, white cords and lace, set in threes on the breast, a scarlet stripe with pewter buttons on a scarlet and green sash, short black boots, and a shako with white lace and cords with a sky blue plume on the side in a red pompon. The mounted chasseurs had the same, but without the pelisse. The hussars had red housings laced white, the chasseurs blue. Later on the pelisse was omitted, the pantaloons had a plain white stripe, and the housings were of imitation leopard fur edged red.

CAVALRY

Organisation

From 1787 heavy cavalry regiments each had three squadrons: each squadron had three companies, and each company had an establishment of 70 men by 1793. Dragoons had 60 men per company. The official establishment was 670 men and 540 horses, but actual strength was often lower. In 1800 the heavy cavalry regiments had 9,878 men, 869 short; the dragoons had 4,129 men, missing 183. This situation became worse, however, after 1802.

From 30 January 1803, all heavy and light cavalry regiments were to have the same organisation and establishment. Each regiment had five

squadrons, of two companies, with a total of ten companies. Each company had one captain, one lieutenant, one ensign, one first sergeant, two second sergeants, four corporals, four second corporals, one trumpeter, four carabiniers or élite troopers, 38 mounted troopers, 13 dismounted troopers. Each regiment had a staff of eight field officers, four standard bearers, a marshal major, a chaplain, a surgeon, a trumpet major, a kettle-drummer, a master saddler, a master armourer and a picador. Light cavalry regiments had the same organisation, lacking only the four standard bearers and the kettle-drummer. In 1808, each of the 24 regiments should have had 700 men, but in fact the total amounted to only 14,440 troopers with 9,500 horses.

Heavy Cavalry Uniforms

At the beginning of the reign of Carlos IV, cavalry regiments had uniforms of various colours as indicated below. All wore hats with yellow or white lace, depending on the unit's button colour, black boots, and housings of the facing colour laced yellow or white. The cape was the same colour as the coat. During the late 1780s and early 1790s regimental uniforms were as set out in Table 1.

Table 1

	Coat	Breeches	Turnbacks	Cuffs/Lapels	Waistcoat	Buttonholes	Buttons
Rey (1538)	Blue	Blue	White	Scarlet	Scarlet	Yellow	Brass
Reina (1703)	Scarlet	Scarlet	Scarlet	Blue	Blue	White	Pewter
Principe (1703)	Blue	Blue	White	Scarlet	Scarlet	White	Pewter
Infante (1642)	Blue	Blue	White	White	White	Yellow	Brass
Borbon (1640)	Blue	Blue	White	Scarlet	Scarlet	-	Pewter
Farnesio (1649)	Scarlet	Scarlet	Scarlet	White	Scarlet	-	Pewter
Alcantara (1656)	White	Green	White	Green	Green	-	Brass
España (1659)	Scarlet	Scarlet	Scarlet	Black	Scarlet	-	Pewter
Algarbe (1701)	Scarlet	Scarlet	Scarlet	Yellow	Scarlet	-	Pewter
Calatrava (1703)	White	Scarlet	White	Scarlet	Scarlet	-	Pewter
Santiago (1703)	Blue	Blue	Scarlet	Scarlet	Buff	-	Pewter
Montesa (1706)	White	Blue	White	Blue	Blue	-	Pewter
Carabineros de Maria Luisa (1793)	Scarlet	Buff	-	Blue, edged with lace	Buff	-	Pewter

Ceuta Garrison Companies fusilier, 1801. Five foot companies equipped as light infantry were permanently posted to this Spanish outpost port on the coast of Morocco. Uniforms were all-blue except for scarlet cuffs and white turnbacks, pewter buttons, a buff ventral cartridge box and half-gaiters. (Anne S.K. Brown Military Collection, Brown University, Providence. Ph: R. Chartrand)

In 1796 the heavy cavalry uniforms were changed considerably. All regiments received white coats with scarlet piping and turnbacks, pewter buttons, buff waistcoats and breeches, bicorn hats edged white, and crimson housings edged with a white lace. The boots were replaced by black dragoon-style long gaiters. The cape was of the coat colour. The 1796 regimental facings were as shown in Table 2.

In 1800 all regiments were ordered to wear blue coats with scarlet piping and turnbacks, pewter buttons, buff waistcoats and breeches, white hat lace, and scarlet housings laced white. The cape was blue like the coat. The facings were however somewhat altered and now were as described in Table 3.

Table 2

	Collar	Cuffs	Lapels
Rey	Violet	Violet	Violet
Reina	Violet	White	Violet
Principe	Violet	Violet	White
Infante	White	Violet	White
Borbon	Scarlet	Scarlet	White
Farnesio	Scarlet	White	White
Alcantara	Green	Green	Green
España	Black	Black	Black
Algarbe	Buff	Scarlet	Lapels
Calatrava	Scarlet	Scarlet	Scarlet
Santiago	Crimson	Crimson	Crimson
Montesa	Blue	Blue	Blue
Carabineros de Maria Luisa	Sky blue	Sky blue	Sky blue

15

In 1802 all heavy cavalry regiments were assigned the same uniform; blue coats with white lapels, crimson-red collar, cuffs, turnbacks and piping edging the lapels, white piping edging the collar, cuffs and turnbacks, blue cuff flaps piped crimson-red, a yellow lion badge at the collar, brass buttons, yellow waistcoats, blue pantaloons with a crimson-red stripe strapped with black leather, bicorns laced yellow with a red plume, and blue housings edged with a yellow lace. This common uniform caused some grumbling in the regiments.

In 1805 regimental uniforms were re-adopted. All regiments had the lion badge at the collar, and cuff buttons shaped as fleurs-de-lis in yellow or white depending on the regimental button, buff waistcoats and breeches, bicorns with white or yellow lace and a red plume, and blue housings edged yellow or white. The 1805 regimental distinctions were as detailed in Table 4.

Ceuta Cavalry Company, trooper, 1801. Also called Ceuta Lancers, the company was formed in 1584 and was thus one of the oldest cavalry formations in the Spanish army. Wearing blue coats and breeches, with scarlet collar, cuffs, lapels, turnbacks and waistcoat, white piping, pewter buttons, white hat lace, and scarlet housings edged white, the men were also armed with lances. (Anne S.K. Brown Military Collection, Brown University, Providence. Ph: R. Chartrand)

Table 3

	Collar	Cuffs	Lapels
Rey	Scarlet	Scarlet	Violet
Reina	Violet	Scarlet	Scarlet
Principe	Scarlet	Scarlet	Scarlet
Infante	White	Violet	White
Borbon	White	White	Scarlet
Farnesio	Scarlet	Scarlet	White
Alcantara	Green	Green	Green
España	Black	Black	Black
Algarbe	Sky blue	Sky blue	Buff
Calatrava	Scarlet	White	Scarlet
Santiago	Crimson	Crimson	Crimson
Montesa	White	Buff	White
Carabineros de Maria Luisa	Sky blue	Sky blue	Sky blue

Table 4

	Collar	Cuffs	Lapels	Piping	Turnbacks	Buttons
Rey	Scarlet	Scarlet	Scarlet	Scarlet	Scarlet	Brass
Reina	Sky blue	Sky blue	Sky blue	Scarlet	Scarlet	Brass
Principe	Scarlet	Scarlet	Scarlet	Scarlet	Scarlet	Pewter
Infante	White	White	White	White	Scarlet	Brass
Borbon	Scarlet	Scarlet	Scarlet	Scarlet	Scarlet	Pewter
Farnesio	Scarlet	Scarlet	Scarlet	Buff	Scarlet	Pewter
Alcantara	Scarlet with buff piping	Scarlet	Buff	Scarlet	Emerald green	Pewter
España	Buff	Crimson with buff piping	Crimson with buff piping	Scarlet	Scarlet	Pewter
Algarve	Buff	Buff	Buff	Scarlet	Scarlet	Pewter
Calatrava	Scarlet	Sky blue	Sky blue	Scarlet	Scarlet	Pewter
Santiago	Crimson	Crimson	Crimson	Scarlet	Scarlet	Pewter
Montesa	Crimson with white piping	Crimson with white piping	White	Scarlet	Scarlet	Pewter

Royal Corps of Artillery gunner, 1801, wearing a blue coat and breeches, with scarlet collar, cuffs and waistcoat, gold lace edging the collar, brass buttons, and a bicorn laced yellow. (Anne S.K. Brown Military Collection, Brown University, Providence. Ph: R. Chartrand)

Dragoons

During the first years of Carlos IV's reign, all dragoon regiments apart from the Rey and Reina had yellow coats without lapels and collars, yellow waistcoats and breeches. Except for Lusitania which had yellow housings laced white, all units had housings of the facing colour edged with lace of the button colour. The regimental uniforms in the late 1780s and early 1790s were as set out in Table 5.

In 1796 the uniforms of the dragoon regiments underwent substantial changes. All regiments had a yellow coat with scarlet turnbacks, pewter buttons, a hat edged with white lace, a white waistcoat and breeches, and yellow housings edged white. All had a yellow cape. The 1796 facings were as shown in Table 6.

The yellow of the coats and capes was changed to green on 9 June 1800. The turnbacks were scarlet and the buttons pewter for all. The waistcoat and breeches were also changed to buff. The housings were green edged with white lace. The regimental facing colours were as set out in Table 7.

Incredibly, the corps of dragoons was abolished in 1803 and the regiments transformed into hussars and mounted chasseurs. Not only did the regiments resent this transformation, but the tactical void left by their absence quickly exposed the futility of this flawed reorganisation.

On 30 January 1805, the dragoon regiments were reinstated and instructed to wear a uniform of a yellow coat, scarlet turnbacks, pewter buttons, white crossed sword and quill pen embroidered at the collar, and white buttonhole lace on the lapels only. The collar, cuffs, cuff flaps and lapels had white piping for all units, and there were four buttons to each cuff flap and vertical pocket flap. The waistcoat and breeches were yellow, and the bicorn hats were laced white with a red plume. The cape was the same colour as the coat. The 1805 facings were as described in Table 8.

Table 5

	Coat	Breeches	Cuffs	Waistcoat	Turnbacks	Buttons	Buttonhole	Hat lace
Rey (1674)	Blue	Blue	Scarlet	Scarlet	White	Brass	Yellow	Yellow
Reina (1735)	Scarlet	Blue	Blue	Blue	White	Brass	Yellow	Yellow
Almansa (1676)	-	-	Blue	-	Yellow	Pewter	-	White
Pavia (1684)	-	-	Scarlet	-	Yellow	Pewter	-	White
Villaviciosa (1689)	-	-	Scarlet	-	Scarlet	Pewter	-	White
Sagunto (1703)	-	-	Scarlet	-	Yellow	Pewter	-	White
Numancia (1707)	-	-	Blue	-	Blue	Brass	-	Yellow
Lusitania (1709)	-	-	Black	-	White	Pewter	-	White

Table 6

	Lapels	Collar	Cuffs	Piping
Rey	Yellow	Violet	Violet	Violet
Reina	Yellow	Sky blue	Sky blue	Sky blue
Almansa	Yellow	Blue	Blue	Blue
Pavia	Yellow	Scarlet	Scarlet	Scarlet
Villaviciosa	Yellow	White	White	White
Sagunto	Yellow	Green	Green	Green
Numancia	Black	Black	Black	Yellow
Lusitania	Yellow	Black	Black	Black

Table 7

	Lapels	Collar	Cuffs	Piping
Rey	Crimson	Crimson	Crimson	Yellow
Reina	Scarlet	Scarlet	Scarlet	Yellow
Almansa	Sky blue	Sky Blue	Sky blue	Scarlet
Pavia	Yellow	Yellow	Yellow	Scarlet
Villaviciosa	Sky blue	Scarlet	Sky blue	Scarlet
Sagunto	Crimson	Yellow	Crimson	Scarlet
Numancia	Green	Yellow	Yellow	Scarlet
Lusitania	Black	Scarlet	Scarlet	Scarlet

RIGHT **Royal Corps of Engineers officer, 1801**, wearing a blue coat and breeches, with red collar, cuffs, turnbacks and waistcoat, silver lace and buttons. (Anne S.K. Brown Military Collection, Brown University, Providence. Ph: R. Chartrand)

FAR RIGHT **Cosmographic staff officer of the Royal Corps of Engineers, 1801**, dressed in a green coat, with scarlet collar, cuffs, lapels, lining, waistcoat and breeches, gold lace edging the lapels, gold epaulettes and buttons, plain hat. (Anne S.K. Brown Military Collection, Brown University, Providence. Ph: R. Chartrand)

Table 8

	Collar	Cuffs/Cuff flaps/ Pocket piping/ Lapels
Rey	Crimson	Crimson
Reina	Scarlet	Scarlet
Almansa	Sky blue	Sky blue
Pavia	Yellow	Yellow
Villaviciosa	Green	Green
Sagunto	Yellow	Green
Numancia	Black	Black
Lusitania	Yellow	Black

A **Spanish line infantry M1801 .69 cal. musket**, with '*a la moda*' lock, and brass mountings. (Natural History Museum of Los Angeles County)

It took a short time, however, for some regiments to revert back to the yellow uniforms. In 1807, the Villaviciosa Dragoons with Romana's corps were often sketched wearing the old green hussar-style uniform.

Mounted Chasseurs

Raised in 1762, the first regiment of Mounted Chasseurs (*Cazadores a Caballo*) was the Voluntarios de España. Its establishment was the same as the line cavalry, and uniforms were the same as line cavalry regiments until 1802. In the 1790s, they wore a green coat with green turnbacks and waistcoat, crimson collar, cuffs and lapels, white lace edging the facings and waistcoat, pewter buttons, buff breeches, high boots, and hats edged white. In 1800 the uniform changed to a blue coat, with green collar and cuffs, yellow lapels, scarlet piping and turnbacks, pewter buttons, white hat lace, and scarlet housings edged white. The regiment was converted into hussars from 1802 until 1805.

In 1803 the mounted chasseur regiments were augmented by the former dragoon regiments of Rey, Reina, Almansa, Pavia, Villaviciosa and Sagunto. All were to have the same uniform; emerald green dolmans and pantaloons, scarlet collar and cuffs, white cords, pewter buttons, a palm and sabre badge, a black leather helmet with a black fur crest, a yellow turban with a brass badge in front and a red plume, and emerald green housings laced white.

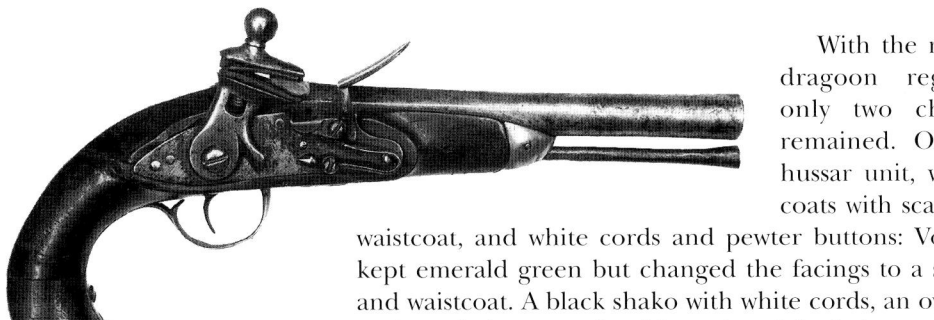

With the reinstatement of the dragoon regiments in 1805, only two chasseurs regiments remained. Olivenza, formerly a hussar unit, wore emerald green coats with scarlet collar, cuffs and waistcoat, and white cords and pewter buttons: Voluntario de España kept emerald green but changed the facings to a sky blue collar, cuffs and waistcoat. A black shako with white cords, an oval white metal plate and a red plume on the side replaced the helmet.

Hussars

In 1795 the Españoles Hussar Regiment was raised with an establishment of 350 men in five squadrons, the first hussar unit in the Spanish army since 1747. Its uniform was a sky blue dolman and pantaloons, 'Corinth grape' (seemingly a reddish hue) dolman collar, cuffs and cords and pelisse, a black mirleton cap with a sky blue wing edged white with a red plume, and a red sash. The pelisse had sky blue cords and was edged with white fur. In 1800, the uniform changed to a light-yellowish buff dolman and breeches, with sky blue collar, cuffs and breeches, white cords, pewter buttons, and a black bearskin busby with a red bag and plume.

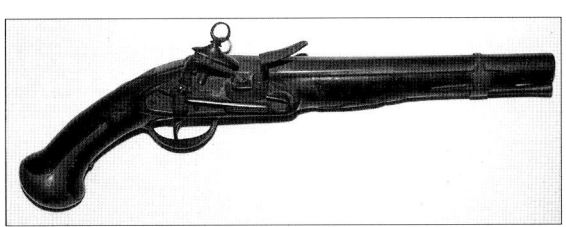

TOP **A Spanish cavalry M1801 .69 cal. pistol, with 'a la moda' lock, and brass mountings. (Natural History Museum of Los Angeles County)**

ABOVE **A Spanish cavalry M1789 .69 cal. pistol with Miquelet lock, and brass mountings. (Gene Autry Western Heritage Museum, Los Angeles)**

In 1803 the number of hussar regiments increased to six, namely the 1st Numancia, 2nd Lusitania, 3rd Olivenza, 4th Voluntario de España, 5th Maria Luisa and 6th Españoles. All were to have the same uniform; a scarlet dolman with sky blue collar and cuffs, sky blue pelisse with scarlet collar and cuffs edged with black fur, sky blue breeches, scarlet and sky blue sash, white cords and a sabre and palm badge at the collar, pewter buttons, a high black cap with a brass oval badge, scarlet wing piped white and red plume, and sky blue housings edged white.

In January 1805 the first four regiments reverted to being dragoons and chasseurs, leaving only two hussar regiments. The Maria Luisa Hussars kept the same uniform. The Españoles Hussars, however, adopted a new uniform consisting of an emerald green dolman with sky blue collar and cuffs, a sky blue pelisse edged with dark fur and with an emerald green collar, white cords and pewter buttons, a sky blue sash with scarlet knots, sky blue pantaloons, a black cap with a brass oval badge, sky blue wing piped white and a red plume, and sky blue housings edged white.

Silver fleur-de-lis button, *c.* 1802–1820. This type of button was worn at the collar of many units from 1802, as well as on the cuffs of line cavalry from 1805. This particular button was found in the southern United States. (Coll. & Ph: John Powell)

LINE INFANTRY

In the early 1790s, each regiment had two service battalions and one depot battalion, each with four companies of fusiliers: the service battalions also had a company of grenadiers each, giving a total establishment of 1,403 men, which was raised to 1,903 for all ranks in 1793. From 26 August 1802 until 1808, each regiment had three battalions: the first battalion had two companies of grenadiers and two of fusiliers, the second and third each had four companies of fusiliers

19

Table 9

	Coatee	Cuffs	Lapels	Collar	Piping	Buttons	Hat
Rey (immemorial)	White	Violet	Violet	Scarlet	Scarlet	Brass	
Reina (1537)	White	Scarlet	White	Scarlet	Scarlet	Brass	
Principe (1537)	White	Violet	Violet	Violet	Violet	Pewter	
Saboya (1537)	White	Black	Black	Black	Black	Pewter	
Corona (1537)	White	Blue	Blue	Blue	Blue	Pewter	
Africa (1559)	White	Black	Black	White	Black	Brass	
Zamora (1580)	White	Black	White	Black	Black	Brass	
Soria (1591)	White	Violet	White	Violet	Violet	Pewter	
Cordoba (1650)	White	Scarlet	Scarlet	Violet	Violet	Brass	
Guadalajara (1657)	White	Scarlet	Scarlet	Scarlet	Scarlet	Pewter	
Sevilla (1657)	White	Scarlet	Black	Black	Scarlet	Brass	
Granada (1657)	White	Buff	Buff	Green	Green	Brass	
Valencia (1658)	White	Scarlet	Scarlet	Buff	Buff	Pewter	
Zaragoza (1660)	White	Green	White	Green	Green	Brass	
España (1660)	White	Green	Green	Green	Green	Brass	
Toledo (1661)	White	Sky blue	Sky blue	Scarlet	Scarlet	Brass	
Mallorca (1682)	White	Scarlet	Scarlet	Buff	Buff	Brass	
Burgos (1694)	White	Violet	Violet	White	Violet	Pewter	
Murcia (1694)	White	Sky blue	White	Sky blue	Sky blue	Brass	
Leon (1694)	White	Scarlet	Scarlet	White	Scarlet	Pewter	
Cantabria (1703)	White	Sky blue	Sky blue	Sky blue	Sky blue	Pewter	
Asturias (1703)	White	Sky blue	Sky blue	White	Sky blue	Brass	
Fijo de Ceuta (1703)	White	Green	White	Green	Green	Pewter	
Navarra (1705)	White	Sky blue	Sky blue	Scarlet	Scarlet	Pewter	
Aragon (1711)	White	Scarlet	Scarlet	Green	Green	Brass	
America (1764)	White	Buff	Buff	Violet	Violet	Pewter	
Princesa (1766)	White	Scarlet	White	White	Scarlet	Brass	
Extremadura (1766)	White	Buff	Buff	Scarlet	Scarlet	Pewter	
Malaga (1791)	White	Buff	Buff	Buff	Buff	Pewter	
Jaen (1793)	White	Black	Black	Scarlet	Scarlet	Pewter	
Ordonnes Militares (1793)	White	Scarlet	White	Scarlet	Green	Pewter	
Voluntarios de Castilla (1793)	White	Crimson	Crimson	Crimson	Crimson	Pewter	Unlaced
Voluntarios del Estado (1794)	Blue coat	Buff	Buff	Blue	Scarlet	Pewter	
Borbon (1796) [1]	Blue coat, with sky blue piping	Scarlet, with white cuff flap with two buttons	Sky blue, with small buttons and sky blue piping	Scarlet, with scarlet piping	-	Brass, with three buttons on pocket flap	Unlaced

[1] This uniform is according to the Spanish Army List. The regiment is also shown in the 1801 plates wearing blue cuff flaps piped scarlet, with scarlet piped white collar, cuffs and turnbacks.

Foreign Infantry

Irlanda (1698, Irish)	White	Scarlet	Scarlet	Scarlet	Green	Pewter	
Hibernia (1709, Irish)	White	Scarlet	Scarlet	Green	Green	Pewter	
Ultonia (1709, Irish)	White	Green	White	Scarlet	Scarlet	Brass	
Kruter (1734, Swiss), Schwaler (from 1796)	Blue coat	Scarlet	Scarlet	Pale yellow	White	Pewter	
San Gall (1742, Swiss), Ruttiman (from 1798)	Blue coat	Scarlet	Scarlet	Scarlet	White	Pewter, double vertical coat pockets	
Reding (1742, Swiss)	Blue coat	Scarlet	Scarlet	Yellow	White	Pewter	
Betschart (1742, Swiss)	Blue coat	Yellow	Yellow	Scarlet	White	Pewter	
Napoles (1752, Italian)	White	Scarlet	Scarlet	Sky blue	Sky blue	Pewter	
Yann (1793, Swiss)	Blue coat	Scarlet	Scarlet	Scarlet	White	Brass	
Courten (1796, Swiss)	Blue coat	Scarlet	Scarlet	Blue	White	Pewter	

A heavy cavalry broadsword with an iron hilt, c. 1800. (Gene Autry Western Heritage Museum, Los Angeles)

giving a total of 12 companies. Each company had one captain, one lieutenant, one sub-lieutenant, one first sergeant, four second sergeants, eight corporals, eight second corporals, three drummers, 60 (in peacetime) or 164 (in wartime) privates. Each battalion had a staff of three field officers, an ensign, a chaplain, a surgeon, a drum major and a master armourer. In 1808, it amounted to 59,000 men including 15,000 foreign soldiers.

Uniforms 1791–1802

Until the last decade of the 18th century, the Spanish line infantry generally wore white single-breasted coats with cuffs, waistcoats and breeches of various colours. Foreign regiments had their own distinctions: Irish regiments wore red coats, the Swiss had blue, and the Italians and Walloons had white. From 1791 considerable changes were made in the uniforms. Short-tailed coatees with lapels replaced the long-tailed coats. The Irish regiments gave up their traditional red coats for white, but the Swiss kept their blue dress and long-tailed coats. All had white waistcoats and breeches. Until 1797 the black felt hats were edged with yellow or white lace (depending on the regimental button colour) and were plain black thereafter. Grenadiers and sappers wore bearskin caps. Black knee-length gaiters were worn for ordinary dress and on campaign, and over-the-knee white gaiters for gala dress and parades. The facings in the 1790s were as set out in Table 9.

The turnbacks were of the coat colour for all except the Swiss regiments. San Gall and Reding were scarlet, Betschart yellow and Yann white. The waistcoat and breeches were of the coat colour, except for the Voluntarios del Estado, Schwaller and Yann regiments which had white in spite of their blue coats. By 1801, it would seem that all Swiss regiments had blue coats with scarlet cuffs, lapels and turnbacks, white piping, and pewter buttons. Collars were red for Ruttiman, Yann and Reding, yellow with a blue tab for Schwaller, and blue for Courteen. All had horizontal pockets with plain cuffs, except for Ruttiman which had a blue cuff flap and vertical pockets. The Swiss regiments had been allowed by special royal permission since 1767 to edge their red Spanish cockades with white.

Uniform Experiments

From 1793, a distinct campaign uniform was introduced for troops deployed against the French. This special dress consisted of a brown coatee with the same facings as on the regular coatee, white turnbacks, a white waistcoat, brown breeches, a round hat turned up with cockade and a headband in yellow or white according to the regimental button. A 'poncho' for cold weather completed the campaign dress. Only partially successful, this campaign dress was shelved by 1796. However, a few units obviously liked the idea and later in the war some regiments had brown campaign uniforms.

Another curious experiment took place in 1800 with the replacement of the bicorn hat with a 'Russian' mitre cap made of the coat cloth and

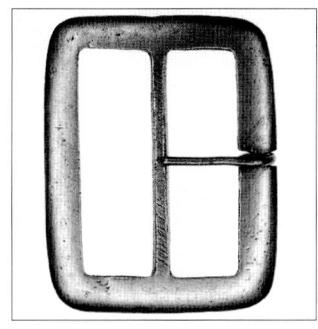

Waistbelt buckle, *c.* 1780–1820. The standard brass buckle used from the 1770s to the 1820s: it may have also been used as a shoulder belt buckle. (Coll. & Ph: John Powell)

Infantry buttons, *c.* 1797–1820. *Top left*: silver button of the Luisiana [Louisiana] colonial regiment. *Top centre and bottom left*: pewter generic infantry button probably post-1808. *Top right and centre bottom*: brass button of the Cuba colonial regiment. *Bottom right*: brass British-made button of the Havana colonial regiment. While it appears to have been the practice from 1797 in some regiments in the Peninsula and in the colonies, buttons were ordered marked with the regimental name on 2 June 1800 for cavalry and on 8 July 1802 for infantry. Provincial militia regiments were to have their buttons stamped with 'Pl de' above their name. All buttons shown were found in the southern United States. (Coll. & Ph: John Powell)

facing colour, with lace, a pompon at the top, and the royal arms on the front. This strange headgear appears to have hardly ever been worn.

On 8 July 1802 a completely new uniform, which was to be the same for all line infantry regiments, was adopted. It consisted of a rather dark sky blue coatee and cuff flaps, with black lapels, collar and cuffs, scarlet turnbacks and piping, brass buttons, yellow fleur-de-lis at the collar, a

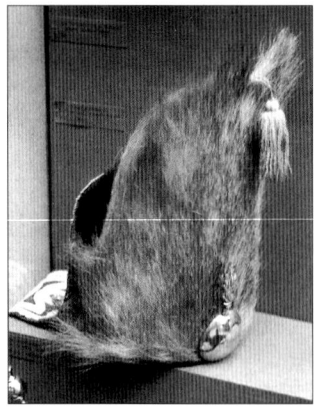

Grenadier officer's cap, c. 1800–1808. A fine quality item of seal fur with a silver tassel and a silver grenade with gold flame in front, red or crimson silk bag elaborately laced and embroidered at the back. (Musée de l'Armée, Paris)

BELOW **Back view.**

Table 10

	Coatee	Cuffs	Lapels	Collar	Piping	Buttons
Rey	White	Violet	Violet	Violet	Violet	Brass
Reina	White	Violet	Violet	Violet	Violet	Pewter
Principe	White	Violet	Violet	White	Violet	Brass
Saboya	White	Black	Black	Black	Black	Brass
Corona	White	Violet	Violet	Violet	Violet	Pewter
Africa	White	Black	Black	White	Black	Brass
Zamora	White	Black	Black	White	Black	Pewter
Soria	White	Violet	Violet	White	Violet	Pewter
Cordoba	White	Scarlet	Scarlet	Scarlet	Scarlet	Brass
Guadalajara	White	Scarlet	Scarlet	Scarlet	Scarlet	Pewter
Sevilla	White	Scarlet	Black	Black	Scarlet	Brass
Granada	White	Sky blue	Sky blue	Sky blue	Sky blue	Brass
Valencia	White	Sky blue	Sky blue	Sky blue	Sky blue	Pewter
Zaragoza	White	Green	Green	Green	Green	Brass
Espait	White	Green	Green	Green	Green	Pewter
Toledo	White	Sky blue	Sky blue	White	Sky blue	Brass
Mallorca	White	Scarlet	Scarlet	White	Scarlet	Brass
Burgos	White	Green	Green	White	Green	Brass
Murcia	White	Sky blue	Sky blue	White	Sky blue	Pewter
Leon	White	Scarlet	Scarlet	White	Scarlet	Pewter
Cantabria	White	White	Sky Blue	Sky blue	Sky blue	Pewter
Asturias	White	Green	Green	White	Green	Pewter
Fijo de Ceuta	White	Green	White	Green	Green	Pewter
Navarra	White	Blue	Blue	Blue	Blue	Brass
Aragon	White	White	Scarlet	Scarlet	Scarlet	Pewter
America	White	Blue	Blue	Blue	Blue	Pewter
Princesa	White	White	Violet	Violet	Violet	Pewter
Extremadura	White	Crimson	Crimson	Crimson	Crimson	Brass
Malaga	White	Blue	Blue	White	Blue	Brass
Jaen	White	Blue	Blue	White	Blue	Pewter
Ordonnes Militares	White	White	Blue	Blue	Blue	Pewter
Voluntarios de Castilla	White	Crimson	Crimson	Crimson	Crimson	Pewter
Voluntarios del Estado	White	Crimson	Crimson	White	Crimson	Brass
Voluntarios de la Corona[1]	White	Crimson	Crimson	White	Crimson	Pewter
Borbon	White	White	Crimson	Crimson	Crimson	Pewter

Foreign Infantry

	Coatee	Cuffs/ Turnbacks	Lapels	Collar	Piping	Buttons
Irlanda (Irish)	Sky blue	Buff	Buff	Buff	Buff	Brass
Hibernia (Irish)	White	Scarlet	Scarlet	Green	Green	Pewter
Ultonia (Irish)	White	Green	White	Scarlet	Scarlet	Pewter
Napoles (Italian)	White	Scarlet	Scarlet	Sky blue	Sky blue	Pewter
Wimpssen (Swiss)	Blue	Scarlet	Scarlet	Scarlet	-	Pewter
Reding (younger and elder) (Swiss)	Blue	Scarlet	Scarlet	Scarlet	-	Pewter
Betschart (Swiss)	Blue	Scarlet	Scarlet	Scarlet	-	Pewter
Traxler (Swiss)	Blue	Scarlet	Scarlet	Scarlet	-	Pewter
Preux (Swiss)	Blue	Scarlet	Scarlet	Blue	White	Pewter

1 This unit originally raised as a light infantry in 1795

RIGHT **Tomas de Morla**, *c.* 1795. De Morla was an outstanding artillery officer, educator and scientist, author of the classic *Tratado de Artilleria* (Treatise of Artillery) and Director-General of Artillery in 1808. He wears a lieutenant-general's uniform: blue coat, scarlet cuffs, collar and lapels, gold buttons and lace, and scarlet sash. (Museo de Artilleria, Segovia)

FAR RIGHT **Salvador del Muro y Salazar, Marquis de Someruelas**, *c.* 1805, wearing a white coat, cuff flap, waistcoat and breeches, with scarlet collar, cuffs, lapels, turnbacks and cuff flap piping, gold buttons and lace, and a scarlet sash. The cuffs have the three laces of a regimental colonel, with two embroidered rows of a lieutenant-general. (Museo de la Ciudad, Havana)

white waistcoat and breeches, a plain bicorn with a red plume, and a bearskin cap for grenadiers and sappers. The cut of the uniform changed: lapels were no longer cut away but were squared and closed down to the waist. Officers had the same uniform but their coat had long tails, gold buttons, epaulettes and lace.

This uniform had no traditional basis in the line infantry and was obviously resented. The historic white or dark blue uniforms were preferred and the regiments cherished their distinctive facing colours.

By 1805 the authorities had recognised their error and on 15 April, the traditional uniforms with regimental facings were restored. The line infantry wore the white coatee with white turnbacks, distinctive facings and piping, brass or pewter buttons according to regiment, a white waistcoat and breeches, a bicorn with a red plume for fusiliers, and a bearskin cap for grenadiers and sappers. The Swiss regiments were in blue and the Irish regiments, which had lost their distinctive red uniforms in 1791, were now to wear sky blue. The 1805 regimental distinctions were as shown in Table 10.

In June and July of 1808, as resistance to the French became stronger, infantry regiments suddenly found themselves with substantial numbers of new recruits, many of whom had not received their full uniforms. The older veteran soldiers wore their dress coatees, while the new soldiers fought their first battle wearing undress linen jackets and forage caps.

LIGHT INFANTRY

Spanish light infantry corps were organised as single battalion units. Each light infantry battalion had an establishment of 801 men from 1792. From 26 August 1802 until 1808, each battalion had six companies: each company had one first captain, one second captain, two lieutenants, two sub-lieutenants, one first sergeant, five second sergeants, eight corporals, eight second corporals, three drummers, and 105 (in peacetime) or 175 (in wartime) privates. Each battalion had a staff of four field officers, an ensign, a chaplain, a surgeon, a drum major and a master armourer. In 1808, the regiments had about 13,600 men.

The early uniforms were varied and bore strong regional features such as the mountaineer's ample *gambeto* coat and the *alpartagas* sandals often worn instead of army shoes. Uniforms from the 1780s to 1802 were as follows.

1st Voluntarios de Aragon (1762): blue gambeto coat and breeches, scarlet cuffs and waistcoat, brass buttons, and hats laced yellow. From *c.* 1794 it consisted of blue coatees, scarlet cuffs, lapels and collar, pewter buttons, white waistcoat and breeches, a brown gambeto coat, hats without lace, and hairnets for the enlisted men. Officers and sergeants had coats instead of coatees.

1st Voluntarios de Cataluna (1762): blue gambeto coat, scarlet cuffs, collar, waistcoat and breeches, brass buttons, hat laced yellow. From *c.* 1794 officers and sergeants wore a blue coat, with yellow cuffs, lapels, collar, turnbacks, gold buttons, white waistcoats and breeches, and an unlaced hat. Corporals and fusiliers wore pale grey gambetos, blue vests or coatees with yellow collars, cuffs and lapels, brass buttons, white waistcoat and breeches.

2nd Voluntarios de Cataluna (1762): blue gambeto coat and breeches, yellow cuffs and waistcoat, pewter buttons, and hats laced white. From *c.* 1794 officers and sergeants wore blue coats, yellow cuffs, lapels, collar, turnbacks, silver buttons, white waistcoat and breeches, and unlaced hats. Corporals and fusiliers wore pale grey gambetos, blue vests or coatees with yellow collar, cuffs and lapels, pewter buttons, white waistcoat and breeches.

Voluntarios de Tarragona (1792): for officers and sergeants, a blue coat, with yellow cuffs, lapels, collar, turnbacks, silver buttons, a white waistcoat and breeches, and an unlaced hat. Corporals and fusiliers had pale grey gambetos, blue vests or coatees with a yellow collar, cuffs and lapels, pewter buttons, white waistcoat and breeches.

Voluntarios de Gerona (1792): for officers and sergeants, blue coats, with yellow cuffs, lapels, collar, turnbacks, silver buttons, white waistcoat and breeches, and an unlaced hat. Corporals and fusiliers wore pale grey gambetos, blue vests or coatees with yellow collars, cuffs and lapels, pewter buttons, white waistcoat and breeches.

2nd Voluntarios de Aragon (1793): a blue coatee, with scarlet cuffs, lapels and collar, brass buttons, a white waistcoat

The castle of Segovia, the superb site of the corps of artillery's military academy.

Brass mortar cast in Sevilla on 20 November 1801, bearing the cipher of Carlos IV.

1. Sergeant, Marine Artillery Brigades
2. Fusilier, Cordoba Regiment
3. Officer Cadiz Urban Militia

B

1. Fusilier, Canarias Battalion
2. Fusilier, Canarias Militia
3. Gunner, Real Artilleria Regiment

1. Fusilier, Yann (Swiss) Regiment
2. Fusilier, Navarra Regiment
3. Trooper, Guardia de Corps, American Company

1. Officer, Infantry
2. Private, Light Infantry
3. Trooper, Mounted Chasseurs

1. Private, Marine Infantry Brigade
2. Corporal, Marine Infantry Brigade, undress
3. Gunner, Marine Artillery Brigade

1. Fusilier, Tercios de Texas
2. Officer, Provincial Militia
3. Trooper, Numancia Dragoon Regiment

and breeches, light brown gambeto coat with buff leather buttons, hat without lace, and hairnets for the enlisted men. Officers and sergeants had coats instead of coatees.

1st Voluntarios de Barcelona (1793): for officers and sergeants, dark bottle green coat, scarlet cuffs and lapels, buff collar, contrasting piping, silver buttons, white waistcoat and breeches. Corporals and fusiliers wore blue gambetos, dark bottle-green coatees with scarlet cuffs and lapels, buff collar, pewter buttons, a white waistcoat and breeches.

Voluntarios de Barbastro (1793): officers and sergeants had blue coats, with scarlet cuffs, lapels, collar, turnbacks, silver buttons, white waistcoat and breeches, and unlaced hats. Corporals and fusiliers wore pale brown ('musk') gambetos, blue vests or coatees with scarlet collars, cuffs and lapels, pewter buttons, white waistcoat and breeches, buff gaiters, unlaced hat and hairnet.

Voluntarios de Valencia (1794): officers and sergeants had blue coats, with white cuffs, lapels, collar, turnbacks, gold buttons, white waistcoat and breeches. Corporals and fusiliers wore blue gambetos, blue vests or coatees with white collars, cuffs and lapels, brass buttons, white waistcoat and breeches.

Voluntarios de la Corona (1795): brown coatees, with sky blue small lapels, cuff flaps, elbow patches and piping, brown waistcoats and ample breeches, round hats turned up on the side with a cockade and loop. By 1800 this had changed to a blue coatee with scarlet collars, cuffs and cuff flaps, white piping, pewter buttons, white waistcoat, long blue breeches, and round hats as before. An 1801 plate shows a hussar-style uniform (see illustration). This unit was transferred to the line infantry in 1802.

In April 1797 there was an attempt to change the uniform of the light infantry units to green, but this was ignored, according to the army regi-sters. From 1800 the light infantry units were all to have blue coatees and green gambetos but it is also doubtful whether this was implemented before the sweeping changes of 1802.

In 1802 the distinctive uniforms were swept away in favour of an entirely new uniform which had no links to the traditional items in Spanish light troops. To quote the 1804 *Estado Militar*: 'The uniform is the same for all, the only distinction being the numbered buttons.' It consisted of a green jacket braided with yellow cords in front (hussar style), scarlet collars, cuffs and cuff flaps all edged with yellow cords, a red sash, a white waistcoat and breeches, buff leather gaiters, *alpargatas* sandals with green ribbons, a black leather 'Tarleton' style cap with a fur crest bearing an oval brass badge in front, and a yellow turban and a green plume. The officers had white pantaloons and half boots. They often wore bicorns instead of caps.

This hussar dress seems to have been better accepted by the light infantrymen than the sky blue uniform of the line infantry. However, its cost and the desire for something more traditional brought revisions.

Troops of Romana's Corps, c. 1807. *Left to right*: drummer, pioneer of the Guadalajara Regiment, colour bearer of the Guadalajara Regiment, back view of an officer of the Guadalajara Regiment, officer of Light Infantry wearing the 1802 hussar uniform. Print after J. Volz. (Anne S.K. Brown Military Collection, Brown University, Providence. Ph: R. Chartrand)

Table 11

	Cuffs	Lapels	Collar	Turnbacks	Piping	Buttons
1st Aragon	Scarlet	Scarlet	Scarlet	Scarlet	White	Pewter
2nd Aragon	Scarlet	Scarlet	Blue	Scarlet	White	Pewter
1st Cataluna	Yellow	Yellow	Yellow	Yellow	Yellow	Brass
2nd Cataluna	Yellow	Yellow	Blue	Yellow	Yellow	Brass
Tarragona	Yellow	Blue	Yellow	Yellow	Yellow	Brass
Gerona	Yellow	Yellow	Yellow	Yellow	Yellow	Pewter
1st Barcelona	Yellow	Blue	Yellow	Yellow	Yellow	Pewter
2nd Barcelona	Yellow	Yellow	Blue	Yellow	Yellow	Pewter
Barbastro	Scarlet	Blue	Scarlet	Scarlet	White	Pewter
Voluntarios de Valencia	Crimson	Crimson	Crimson	Crimson	White	Pewter
Voluntarios de Navarra (1802)	Crimson	Blue	Crimson	Crimson	White	Pewter
Campo Mayor (1802)	Crimson	Crimson	Blue	Crimson	White	Pewter

Engineers and artillery of Romana's Corps, 1807. An officer of engineers and an officer of artillery stand near a field gun, both in their corps uniforms, but the engineer has a white waistcoat and the artillery officer's blue waistcoat is piped scarlet. Lounging on the ground are, at left, a sapper having a drink from a tin canteen, and, in the foreground, a gunner seen from the back revealing details of the coatee's vertical pocket flaps (piped red) and turnbacks. Print after J. Volz. (Anne S.K. Brown Military Collection, Brown University, Providence. Ph: R. Chartrand)

On 15 April 1805 the green hussar style dress was ordered to be replaced by a more standard uniform. It consisted of a blue coatee with lapels, cuffs, collar, piping and turnbacks of distinctive battalion facing colours, white waistcoats and breeches, black gaiters and shoes, a bicorn with green plume and a white cockade loop. Black shakos were also issued and are shown on some soldiers in Romana's Corps. They had cords, an oval plate in front and a green plume on the left side. The gambeto was brown with red collars and cuffs. The 1805 battalion distinctions were as detailed in Table 11.

Texas Spanish *Tercios*

This corps of Texas Spanish *Tercios* (*Tercios Espanoles de Tejas*) was raised in Spain from 6 August 1804 to reinforce the colony of Texas.[3] Officially, it was to consist of four light infantry and four cavalry *tercios*, each of three companies. However, it actually consisted of two light infantry battalion-like *tercios*, while the cavalry was apparently never raised as its existence is unrecorded. In 1808 the corps was stationed in Cadiz and had not been sent overseas. Attached to Reding's Army of Andalucia, it parti-cipated in defeating the French at Bailen in July. On 12 August, both *tercios* were transformed into the Batallon de Cazadores de Bailen and the Batallon de Cazadores de Las Navas de Tolosa.

The infantry uniform was blue coatees and breeches, with scarlet collars, cuffs, lapels and turnbacks, brass buttons, yellow lace edging the collar and lapels, and a silver collar badge bearing the two hemispheres between the pillars of Hercules with gold scrolls.

Independent Companies

There were some 21 independent companies. Some were light infantry *escopeteros* mountaineers,

---

[3] Spanish infantry regiment-like formations were referred to as *tercios* during the 16th and 17th centuries. This name was later occasionally used for special formations, such as this corps.

so named because they were armed with the short and sturdy *escopeta* muskets. Others served as coast guards on the coast south of Granada (basically today's Costa del Sol), which was always subject to opportunist raids by pirates from nearby North Africa. Other companies, including cavalry, were in the Spanish enclaves in Morocco at Ceuta and Melilla. Their uniforms varied and could have a regional style. The two companies of Escopeteros de Andalucia, for example, wore blue coats, waistcoats and breeches, scarlet cuffs and pewter buttons. The 11 Costa de Granada companies had blue uniforms with scarlet cuffs and lapels, buff collars and piping, and brass buttons. The company of Arab light cavalry at Ceuta, the *Moros Mogataces*, were dressed in Arab costume. The Spanish cavalry company of Ceuta Lancers, a corps raised in 1584, had, in 1807, a blue coat and breeches, red collars, cuffs, turnbacks, piping and waistcoats, brass buttons, yellow aiguillettes, hats laced yellow, high black boots, blue housings edged with a broad and a very narrow yellow lace, and were armed with lances, swords and carbines.

Provincial Militias

The Provincial Militias (*Milicias Provinciales*) were a reserve based on limited drafts made in rural Spain, somewhat like the Royal Militia in France (see *Louis XV's Army (2) French Infantry*, MAA 302). They amounted to 42 regiments of one battalion each in the peninsula, and one regiment of two battalions in Mallorca. There was also a battalion of militia in the Canary Islands. Each regiment was named after its area of origin. The militia grenadiers were gathered in four divisions of two battalions each. In wartime or in national emergencies the provincial militias were embodied for full-time military service, usually garrison duties. They were generally more popular among civilians than the regular troops, and their officers were recruited from the gentry in the area where the regiment was drafted. In 1808 the actual strength of the provincial regiments was about 550 men per battalion amounting to about 30,000 troops in total.

The provincial militias all had the same uniform. At the beginning of the reign of Carlos IV, it consisted of a blue coat, with blue turnbacks, waistcoat and breeches, scarlet collars, cuffs and lapels, and brass buttons. The waistcoat and breeches were changed to white in some or all units in about 1796. From 1805 the uniform was changed to a white coatee, with scarlet cuffs, cuff flaps, lapels, collar and turnbacks, brass buttons, white waistcoat and breeches. Fusiliers had hats and grenadiers bearskin caps as in the line infantry. In 1808, with an influx of new recruits to fight the French, uniform clothing became scarce and in the Grenaderos Provinciales de Andalucia, which fought at Bailen, half of the men were reported in full dress with bearskin caps, the rest in fatigue jackets with forage caps.

'A Major of Miners' and personnel of the Regiment of Sappers and Miners, Romana's Corps, 1807. The officer is actually a captain acting as major from the Royal Corps of Engineers and is shown in the corps uniform, but wears a major's single lace around the cuffs denoting his temporary appointment, and a pair of captain's epaulettes. His lapels and collar are shown as a dark violet velvet. He sports non-regulation hussar-style breeches with silver laces, and hussar boots edged silver. The sappers are in the correct regimental uniform and equipment.
A drummer in a red coatee is in the right background. Print after C. Suhr. (Anne S.K. Brown Military Collection, Brown University, Providence. Ph: R. Chartrand)

Urban Militia

The *Milicias Urbanas* consisted of 114 independent companies in 13 municipalities. Cadiz had 20 companies, Puerto Santa Maria nine, Campo Gibraltar 13, Cartagena nine, Ceuta five, Badajos 14, Albuquerque eight, Alcantara six, Alconchel one, Valencia de Alcantara seven, La Coruña 12, Ciudad Rodrigo six, and Tarifa four. These companies were the urban equivalent of the rural provincial regiments, but they were not mobilised in 1808. Their uniforms varied widely. In 1808, for example, the companies of La Coruña and Cartagena wore a blue coat, with white collars, cuffs, lapels, turnbacks, piping, waistcoat and breeches, brass buttons. Those at Badajos, Valencia de Alcantara and Albuquerque had a blue coat, with scarlet lapels and turnbacks, buff collars and cuffs, white waistcoats and breeches, pewter buttons. Troops in Cadiz wore blue coats, with white collars, cuffs, lapels, turnbacks, piping, waistcoat and breeches, brass buttons, and gold lace edging the collar, cuffs and lapels. Uniforms in Alcantara were white with green cuffs and lapels and black collar, etc.

Émigré Corps

As revolution raged in France, nobles and royalists sought refuge in Spain. From May 1793, units of émigrés were raised and most saw much action. Following the end of hostilities with France by the Treaty of Basel on 22 July 1795, the three remaining corps were amalgamated to form the Borbon Infantry Regiment in April 1796. The units were as follows.

Légion de Saint-Simon: raised in June 1793, it was also known as the Légion Royale des Pyrénées, and probably had six companies of 100 men each including one of grenadiers and one of gentlemen volunteers. They fought in the western Pyrenees and Navarra. It was incorporated into the Borbon regiment in 1796.

Légion de la Reine: raised from early 1793, the Queen's Legion had a light infantry battalion with six companies including grenadiers and chasseurs, and a three-company hussar squadron which served on foot that was disbanded in mid-1794. First known as Légion de Pannetier, it became the Légion Catholique et Royale des Pyrénées in January 1794 and the Légion de la Reine in July. Having served in Roussillon, Provence and north-eastern Spain, it moved to Andalucia and was incorporated into the new Borbon Regiment in 1796.

According to the memoirs of one of its officers, the Marquis de Franglieu, the uniform of the infantry comprised white coatees, with scarlet collars, cuffs, lapels and piping, pewter buttons, white waistcoats and pantaloons, and black half-gaiters. The grenadier company was 'magnificent' in its regulation uniform. The chasseurs had 'a small round hat edged with white, turned up on the side, with a white cockade loop, and a green aigrette'.

Royal-Provence: this was an infantry regiment raised in November 1793 during the Anglo-

Grenadiers of the Zamora Regiment with an officer of the Catalonian Light Infantry, Romana's Corps, 1807. The grenadiers of the Zamora Regiment all have their tall black bearskin caps, white uniforms with black lapels, cuffs and cuff flaps, pewter buttons, white laces on the cuffs and a white metal match case on the cartridge box belt which also distinguished grenadiers. To the left is a drummer wearing the king's livery: blue coatee with scarlet collar, cuffs, cuff flaps, lapels and turnbacks edged with the white chain on crimson lace. The drummer's cap badge is scarlet instead of black. The grenadier officer is a captain as he has two silver epaulettes; he wears a gilt gorget with scarlet rosettes. The Catalonian officer wears the 1802 green hussar-style uniform with scarlet collar, cuffs and sash, gold buttons, cords, lace and epaulettes and a large black bicorn with a narrow gold cockade loop and a small red cockade. Print after C. Suhr. (Anne S.K. Brown Military Collection, Brown University, Providence. Ph: R. Chartrand)

Soldiers of Romana's Corps playing cards in camp, 1807. This illustration provides a superb glimpse of the Spanish infantrymen's casual wear. At left, a light infantryman wears the 1802 hussar uniform partly covered by a black cloak; seated below and partly visible is another light infantryman also in the 1802 uniform – note the light brown-edged green gaiters and the sandals. Standing in the background is a soldier of the Asturias Regiment in an undress white fatigue cap with a green turn-up and piping, and a white fatigue jacket with green cords stitched at the shoulders. Next to him, a light infantryman in the 1802 uniform and another man who might be a civilian sutler with a chequered scarf on his head, a light grey blanket with red stripes, a sleeveless green vest, a red sash, brown breeches, and white stockings with red ribbons. Seated at centre is a soldier wearing a bicorn with a red plume, a blue coat with red collar, cuffs, cuff flaps, lapels and shoulder strap, and fleur-de-lis at the collar. Just behind, is a grenadier of the Zamora Regiment with a white fatigue cap with a black turn-up and white grenades, black piping, a white fatigue jacket with black cords stitched at the shoulders, and a red sash. Playing in the foreground, a member of the Guadalajara Regiment wearing a white fatigue cap with a red turn-up and piping, and a white fatigue jacket with red cords at the shoulders, and red sash. The drum is brass with a blue hoop. Print after C. Suhr. (Anne S.K. Brown Military Collection, Brown University, Providence. Ph: R. Chartrand)

Spanish occupation of Toulon. All of its recruits were evacuated to Spain on 21 December and incorporated into the Légion de la Reine in June 1794. Its uniform was to consist of a white coat, collar, lining, waistcoat and breeches, blue lapels and cuffs, and brass buttons.

Royal-Roussillon: this was an infantry regiment formed without royal approbation in Barcelona in January 1794. Recruiting proved difficult and the men enlisted undisciplined. In June over 170 soldiers were killed or wounded in a general riot with Spanish civilians. It was incorporated into the Légion de la Reine in July 1796.

Vallespir: a battalion raised from mountaineers in Roussillon in April 1793, it was renamed 'de la Frontière' (Frontier) battalion in 1794. It campaigned in Roussillon and Catalonia, and was incorporated into the Borbon in 1796.

SPECIALISTS AND AUXILIARY FORCES

Royal Corps of Artillery

The *Real Cuerpo de Artilleria* was organised as a corps in 1710. It consisted of specialist officers assisted by a group of Artillery General Staff (*Estado Mayor de Artilleria*) officers, and a large and varied establishment in Europe and of many other units of the corps posted in the overseas colonies. The corps in the peninsula had five battalions, which was raised to six in 1793. Reorganised into five regiments in 1802, two companies of horse artillery were also created per regiment. The corps was reduced to four regiments in 1806. Each had two battalions and each battalion had four companies of foot and one of horse artillery amounting to 40 batteries with a theoretical 240 guns. There were also 15 companies of regular garrison artillery to serve fortress artillery, five companies of artisans (*obreros de maestranza*) and an establishment of invalids. The corps oversaw 74 companies of disciplined militia artillery in various locations in Spain, and four of urban militia artillery in Cartagena, Cadiz, La Coruña and San Sebastian. It was also responsible for 150 Gentlemen-Cadets at the Artillery Military Academy housed in the Alcazar castle at Segovia.

The quality of the officers, the men and their guns was generally considered quite good, but the proportion of artillery to the rest of the army was insufficient by 1807–1808. Some batteries actually had only four rather than the six guns called for on the establishment. By 1808 the movement of the guns was very slow and still mainly dependent on

Infantry grenadiers and sappers of Romana's Corps in Denmark, 1807. *Left to right*: a grenadier of the Guadalajara Regiment in the 1805 white faced scarlet uniform, a sapper in the 1802 sky blue and black piped scarlet uniform, a sapper of the Asturias Regiment in the 1805 white faced green uniform, a grenadier in the 1802 sky blue uniform. Print after C. Suhr. (Anne S.K. Brown Military Collection, Brown University, Providence. Ph: R. Chartrand)

inadequate hired mule trains. This had been normal in Europe during the 1790s, but Napoleon's creation of militarised artillery trains put the Spanish army at a disadvantage.

The corps uniform in the 1790s consisted of blue coats and breeches, with double vertical pocket flaps, scarlet collars, cuffs, lining, piping and waistcoats, gold lace edging the collar, brass buttons, and bicorns laced yellow. From July 1802 the men were issued a short-tailed coatee, with black lapels piped scarlet buttonholes laced yellow,[4] blue cuff flaps with three buttons (there was no more lace at the collar, but a gold flaming bomb badge was added from 1 April 1804), plain bicorns with red plumes and yellow cords. In 1805 the lapels were changed to blue piped scarlet, and the hats again had a yellow lace edging with the red plume.

The Military Academy cadets in Segovia wore the same uniform as the officers except that they had a short-tailed coatee instead of a coat, and gold aiguillettes instead of epaulettes.

The horse artillery companies had uniforms of the same colours as the foot artillery, but wore pantaloons strapped with leather and a red stripe to each side, black half-boots, a black shako with yellow cords, a red plume at the side, an oval brass plate in front and a red cockade below. Officers wore coatees and shakos, their breeches and hussar-style boot tops having gold lace, and blue housings edged with a broad yellow or gold lace.

The companies of artisans had blue jackets and pantaloons, scarlet collars piped white, scarlet cuffs and piping in front, brass buttons, and round hats.

Officers had a long-tailed coat with four buttons on the cuff flap, gold buttons, lace, collar badge and epaulettes. Off duty, the officers often wore white waistcoats and breeches.

The officers of the Artillery General Staff wore a different uniform comprising green coats, violet stand-and-fall collars, cuffs and lapels, gold lace edging collar and cuffs, scarlet turnbacks, gold buttons, white waistcoats and breeches, gold laced hat with red plume. A gold flaming bomb badge was added at the collar from April 1804. The undress coat, introduced from March 1805, had green facings instead of violet.

Royal Corps of Engineers

The *Real Cuerpo de Ingenieros* was organised as a corps in 1711, with personnel posted in all parts of the peninsula, outlying islands and on all the colonies. There were about 170 officers in the peninsula, including eight generals each of whom headed a segment of the corps. While competent in all aspects of military engineering, the corps' work in coastal fortifications, both at home and in the colonies and especially in Cuba was renowned.

---

[4] Some secondary sources mention that red lapels were added in *c.* 1793 but, as primary sources consulted neither mention this nor show them, it is unlikely that the regular artillery had them. This could be a confusion with the militia artillery which was allowed red lapels.

Troops of Romana's Corps in Denmark, 1807. *Left to right*: mounted and dismounted troopers of the Rey Cavalry Regiment with large bicorns laced white, blue coats with scarlet collar and turnbacks, white or buff breeches, red housings laced white, blue cape; a light infantryman wearing a hairnet in an all-green undress trimmed with white tape; a trooper of the Almanza Dragoons in yellow undress with blue collar and cuffs, white shoulder laces; a grenadier in white faced with scarlet, and a chaplain dressed completely in black mounted on a mule with blue laced white housings. (Private collection)

From 1796 there was also a group of corps General Staff officers within the corps, first called *Cosmografos de Estado* and later *Estado Mayor de Ingenerios* who were distinct and had a different uniform. From 1803, engineer cadets were trained at Alcala de Henarès. The Royal Regiment of Sappers and Miners (see below) was led by engineer officers.

Traditionally, the engineers' uniform colour followed fairly closely that of the artillery but they used silver buttons and lace instead of gold and were allowed, like the Royal Guard, to put silver lace on their coats and waistcoats. Thus, in the 1790s, the uniform was a blue coat and breeches, scarlet collars, cuffs, lining and breeches, silver buttons, silver lace edging the collar only in undress, and broad lace edging the coat in full dress, narrow silver lace edging the waistcoat in full dress and no lace in ordinary dress, and a silver laced hat. In 1802 the uniform was changed to a blue coat, with scarlet collars, cuffs and turnbacks, black velvet lapels with silver buttonhole lace, double vertical pocket flaps piped scarlet, silver buttons, and a hat laced silver with a red plume. The silver turret was added to the collar in 1804. In 1805, the colour of the lapels and collar was changed to violet velvet piped white.

The officers of the Engineer General Staff wore a different uniform; a green coat, scarlet collar, cuffs, lapels, lining, waistcoat and breeches, gold lace edging the lapels, gold epaulettes and buttons, and a plain hat. The facings were probably changed to those of the corps in 1802, and in 1805. The Army Register for 1808 mentions violet collars, cuffs and lapels edged with gold lace, a turret badge at the collar, scarlet turnbacks, gold buttons, white waistcoats and breeches.

Royal Regiment of Sappers and Miners

The *Regimiento Real de Zapadores-Minadores* was organised as a two-battalion regiment on 5 September 1802, each battalion having four companies of sappers (*zapadores*) and one of miners (*minadores*). Each company had an establishment of five officers and 120 men.

The uniform was the same colours as that of the engineers; a blue coatee with black then, from 1805, violet collars and lapels with white buttonhole lace and a white turret badge on the collar from 1804, red cuffs and turnbacks, white piping edging collars, cuffs, lapels and turnbacks, red piping edging the horizontal pocket flaps, blue tight pantaloons, short black gaiters, a black leather helmet with a black fur crest and a white metal oval badge in front, a white turban, and a red plume. They were armed with muskets, bayonets and hangers, and white accoutrements leather ventral cartridge boxes, tan leather aprons and shovels. The corps' history mentions that the miners had three white laces on each cuff as a distinction. According to a print by Suhr, drummers wore red coatees with violet collars, cuffs, wings and apparently lapels, and they carried brass drums with white hoops.

Corps of Invalids

This consisted of 41 companies of old soldiers fit for garrison and police duties in various forts and cities in the kingdom, and 26 companies of incapacitated invalids. Their uniform was a blue coat with blue collars, lapels and breeches, white cuffs, turnbacks and waistcoat, pewter buttons, and white hat lace (present in 1801). Six years later, no lapels or hat lace can be seen.

Medical Corps

The Spanish army's medical services consisted of over 200 surgeons, doctors and other staff. The corps was divided into surgeons serving with the army regiments and *Medicos* serving in military hospitals. The uniform was a blue coat and breeches, scarlet collars, cuffs, lining and waistcoat, silver buttons and lace for the surgeons with the regiments. Hospital medical officers wore the same uniform with buff waistcoats and breeches. The silver lace bordered the collar, cuffs, pocket flaps, front of coat, waistcoat and buttonholes. Rank was denoted by the number of buttonhole laces on the cuffs. Army surgeons had, for a surgeon-major four laces, a surgeon *consultor* three, a first adjutant two and a second adjutant one lace. Hospital staff had, for a *medico-mayor* four laces, a *consultor* three, a first adjutant two and a second adjutant one.

Military Chaplains

Spain was traditionally a deeply religious society with an unwavering attachment to the Roman Catholic faith. Army chaplains were found in many units and corps, led by a vicar general and his secretariat, striving to care for the soldiers' souls. The army did not have a distinctive uniform for chaplains at this time. They wore, in principle, the dress of their religious orders. However, German illustrations of Romana's corps in north Germany during 1807 show chaplains in more practical dress consisting of an all-black coat, waistcoat, breeches and stockings, black buttons and black buttonhole twist cord, sometimes in the shape of a lily, and a black bicorn with a black cockade loop. The only colourful items were the red cockade and the silver cross hanging on a silver chain.

Royal Veterinary School

The *Real Escuela de Veterinaria* was created in 1791 to train specialists in the care of cavalry horses. It consisted of a commandant, two subalterns, three sergeants, three corporals and 70 *alumnos*. The uniform was a blue coat, lining and breeches, scarlet collars and waistcoats, gold buttons. Professors had a

Spanish troops at the siege of Stralsund, which the Swedish surrendered on 18 August 1807. *Left to right*: a soldier in white undress; a grenadier; a sapper and a fusilier of the Guadalajara Regiment in white faced red; a fusilier of the Zamora Regiment in white faced black; a fusilier of the Catalonian Light Infantry in the green hussar dress; a trooper of the Villaviciosa Dragoons in the green light cavalry uniform; a trooper of the Algarve Cavalry Regiment in blue with buff facings piped scarlet; two officers of the Zamora and Guadalajara regiments; and a drummer or trumpeter seen from the back in a blue coat with red and white livery lace. (Private collection)

gold lace at the collar and cuffs with a gold-laced hat; sub-professors had lace at the collar only; and *alumnos* had no lace and a plain hat.

WEAPONS

From the beginning of the 18th century, the Spanish army was strongly influenced by French systems of armament. The calibres were similar and the general appearance of the weapons followed those of the French army, although increasingly distinct features were adopted towards the end of the 18th century. Unlike the French, the Spanish muskets had brass furnishings and eventually in 1789 sturdy Miquelet-style locks were introduced, followed by the smaller '*a la moda*' locks from 1801, and the French lock in 1807.

Infantry fusiliers were armed with a musket and bayonet, and equipped with a cartridge box with its own shoulder belt and bayonet scabbard also with its own shoulder belt. The widely used M1757 infantry musket was produced until the M1789 was introduced, but was probably still carried by many units. The next model came in 1807 and was generally similar to the French infantry musket except for the brass furnishings, but few were made and issued before 1808.

Infantry grenadiers had the same arms and also carried a short sabre with its scabbard slung below the bayonet scabbard.

Light infantry fusiliers had a musket and bayonet and were equipped with a cartridge box with its own shoulder belt: the waistbelt supported a ventral cartridge box, as well as the bayonet. From about 1805 some units were equipped as fusiliers, without a ventral cartridge box.

Cazadores or chasseurs light infantry units were usually armed with a shorter musket or Catalonian style *escopeta* musket with bayonet, a cartridge box on the shoulder belt, and the ventral cartridge box on a waistbelt.

Sergeants were armed as grenadiers, with, in addition, a short sabre.

Infantry officers were armed with sword, musket and bayonet until 1795, when they were ordered to have only a sword or a sabre. On campaign, they often equipped themselves with pistols.

Heavy cavalry troopers had a heavy straight-bladed sabre, a pair of pistols and a carbine. They had a small cartridge box carried on a shoulder belt slung over the right shoulder, and a carbine belt with its hook was slung over the left shoulder, with a waistbelt for the sabre.

Dragoons had a somewhat lighter 'dragoon sabre', a dragoon musket and a pair of pistols. They had a small cartridge box carried on a shoulder belt slung over the right shoulder; the musket was slung by its sling over the left shoulder and the sabre hung from the waistbelt.

Hussars and mounted chasseurs had a curved light cavalry sabre, a pair of pistols and a carbine. They had a small cartridge box carried on a shoulder belt slung over the right shoulder, a carbine belt with its hook slung over the left shoulder, and a waistbelt for the sabre. Hussars also had sabretaches. Some mounted chasseurs are also shown with ventral boxes and carbines slung over the left shoulder. Cavalry NCOs and officers were armed as their men except for carbines.

Besides their artillery equipment, artillerymen were armed with a short musket, bayonet and short sabre. Cartridge boxes, bayonets and

Lusitania Dragoon Regiment, trooper, 1807–1808. This regiment was in Madrid from March 1808. During the revolt of 2 May, its men tried to calm and encourage the populace to return home to avoid the French repression and in June, it was ordered to march with General Moncey's French troops to occupy Valencia. On the way, a detachment deserted to join the insurgents in Sevilla, and in July most of the regiment did the same and went to Badajos in Estremadura. The regiment received its yellow and black uniform in 1807 and early 1808. (After a plate in J.A. Rivas Octavio, *Lusitania*, Valencia, 1994)

sabre scabbards hung from a shoulder belt. From 1802 the bayonet and sabre scabbards were carried on a waistbelt.

Sappers and miners were armed with a regular infantry musket, bayonet and short sabre. They were equipped with a ventral cartridge box, with bayonet and sabre scabbards carried on a waistbelt.

Artillery

The Spanish artillery *matériel* at the time of the Napoleonic Wars consisted of a mixture of the French Gribeauval system, adopted in 1783, and some older Vallières system ordnance dating back to 1743. The new Gribeauval system guns were generally used as field guns of 4-, 8- and 12-pdrs. while the older pieces of 16- and 24-pdrs. were frequently employed as siege or garrison guns. There were also 8-in. bore howitzers, and 8-, 10- and 12-in. mortars. This ordnance was cast at the royal arsenals at Sevilla and Barcelona, although the brass often came from the New World as many surviving examples are marked *cobres de Mejico* or *cobres de America*.

Until the 1780s and early 1790s, artillery carriages were often of the Vallières system, but with somewhat more ornate and elaborate ironwork than their French counterparts. These older patterns were sometimes painted red or just oiled. The Gribeauval-pattern carriages became numerous from the early 1790s and were painted light blue. Enough wood (especially mahogany, cedar, black cottonwood and zapodilla) to make 1,000 carriages with wheels and mountings was to be delivered to Spain annually from Central America.

THE NAVY

At the end of the 18th century, Spain had a powerful navy which had been built up during the reign of King Carlos III at the large naval bases of Ferrol, Cadiz, and Cartagena in Spain, and Havana in Cuba. Especially notable were the superb ships-of-the-line, including the world's largest vessel, the *Santisimo Trinidad*, which could carry up to 130 guns. The Spanish navy was then the third largest in the world, after Britain and France. The wars of the French Revolution and the rise of Napoleon saw a gradual decline in the fleets of France and Spain. The 1805 British victory at Trafalgar over the French and Spanish left the Spanish fleet a mere shadow of its former strength.

Since the early 18th century, officers of the Spanish navy had worn a uniform of blue faced red. At the time of the Napoleonic Wars, this consisted of a blue coat with scarlet collars, cuffs, lapels and turnbacks, a gold lace edging the collar, cuffs and lapels, and trimmed with gold buttons bearing a crowned anchor, white waistcoats and breeches or pantaloons, black half-boots and black sword belt, a bicorn edged with gold and with a red cockade. There was also an undress uniform which was to be worn only while on board ship and in the arsenals. This uniform consisted of a single-breasted,

---

One of the surprises for the French at the battle of Bailen in 1808 was the appearance and charge of '*Garrochistas*' or Lancers of Andalucia. They were formed in May and June from cattlemen who were always in the saddle wielding lances to prod bulls. Detachments from Echevarri, Carmona, Jerez de la Frontera and Utrera were with the army of Andalucia which trapped Gen. Dupont. These volunteer lancers wore their own colourful Andalusian riding and working dress which was generally a wide-brimmed hat of straw or felt over a red head scarf and often a net for the hair, a green velvet jacket often elaborately embroidered in black, leather breeches which were also decorated, and tan boots.

all-blue coat with gold buttons, red waistcoat, blue pantaloons and an unlaced hat.

Rank badges in the Spanish navy were similar to those of the land forces. Captains of ships-of-the-line had three gold laces on each cuff, captains of frigates had two, lieutenants of ships-of-the-line had one, lieutenants of frigates had gold epaulettes on each shoulder, ensigns of ships-of-the-line had one on the right shoulder, and ensigns of frigates had one on the left.

A rank peculiar to the Spanish navy was that of brigadier, whose uniform was similar to that of captain of a ship-of-the-line, but with a broad silver twisted lace on the cuffs, worn above the three gold laces. Admirals had uniforms similar to generals in the army, except they had buttons with a crowned anchor on.

Marines

The sea-soldiers were based in the three large naval bases of Ferrol, Cartagena and Cadiz. The *Infanteria de Marina* (marine infantry) during this period had an establishment of over 12,000 men divided into 12 battalions, each having six companies. This was reduced to only four battalions on 2 December 1806. The *Real Cuerpo de Artilleria de Marina* (marine artillery) had an establishment of over 3,000 men divided into 20 *brigadas* (brigades) but was also much reduced after Trafalgar.

At the beginning of Carlos IV's reign, the brigades of marine infantry had an all-blue uniform with scarlet cuffs, brass buttons, yellow hat lace and bearskin caps for marine grenadiers. From 1802, scarlet lapels and turnbacks, blue cuff flaps and a yellow anchor at the collar were added, with white waistcoats and breeches in summer, blue in winter, and a plain bicorn with a yellow cockade loop. They also had a brown working uniform, with scarlet collars, cuffs and piping, an anchor badge at the collar, and a brown fatigue cap with a scarlet turnup.

Marine artillery initially had a blue uniform with scarlet collars, cuffs, lapels and waistcoats, brass buttons, and yellow hat lace. From 1802 they had blue piped scarlet lapels and cuff flaps, long scarlet turnbacks, a yellow flaming bomb over anchor badge at the collar, white waistcoats and breeches in summer, blue in winter, a plain bicorn with yellow cockade loop. There was a brown undress uniform with scarlet collars, cuffs and lining, with a badge at the collar.

The uniform of the drummers was blue faced scarlet, with the royal livery lace as for other troops. Accoutrements were officially white, but some period sources show them as black from 1802. There were a great many variations and additional details to the above uniforms, especially in colonial stations. For instance, in Buenos Aires during 1807, six marine companies of 60 men each were raised locally to join the sailors and veteran marines. These troops were part of the forces which managed to defeat the British invasion force. They wore a round hat with a red plume, dark blue jackets with red cuffs and collars and three rows of buttons, and dark blue trousers.

The Invalids of the navy were older marines employed to guard arsenals. They wore blue coats, collar, turnbacks, waistcoat and breeches, white cuffs, brass buttons, and an unlaced bicorn.

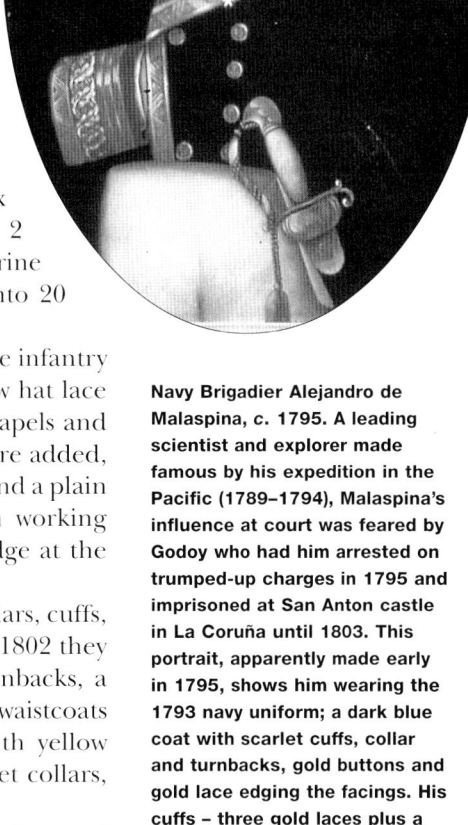

Navy Brigadier Alejandro de Malaspina, c. 1795. A leading scientist and explorer made famous by his expedition in the Pacific (1789–1794), Malaspina's influence at court was feared by Godoy who had him arrested on trumped-up charges in 1795 and imprisoned at San Anton castle in La Coruña until 1803. This portrait, apparently made early in 1795, shows him wearing the 1793 navy uniform; a dark blue coat with scarlet cuffs, collar and turnbacks, gold buttons and gold lace edging the facings. His cuffs – three gold laces plus a silver twisted lace – indicate his rank. (Museo Naval, Madrid)

There were many other uniforms worn in the navy by specialists and administrative officers. Naval engineers had the same uniform as naval officers. From 1784, the Navy Administration uniforms were basically the same as those of the Army Administration, but used gold rather than silver lace. From about 1793 navy surgeons wore blue coats and breeches, with scarlet collars, cuffs, turnbacks and waistcoat, gold buttons and lace edging the coat and facings. Surgeon-majors had three gold buttonhole cuff laces, while surgeons first class had two, and so on.

From 5 November 1798 navy chaplains wore blue coats with blue cloth buttons, with violet cuffs, no collar or lapels, a black or white religious collar, a black waistcoat, breeches with black cloth buttons, and no epaulettes. Religious orders' habits could be worn instead.

From 6 October 1806 navy auditors wore the same uniform as army auditors, but with a gold-embroidered anchor at the collar.

SELECT BIBLIOGRAPHY

Archives: Archivo General de Simancas, Guerra Moderna; Museo Naval (Madrid), manuscript collections.

Albi de la Cuesta, Julio, et al, *Un Eco de Clarines: la Caballería Española*, Madrid, 1992.
Bueno, José Maria, *El Ejercito y la Armada en 1808*, Malaga, 1982.
Bueno, José Maria, *Soldados de España*, Malaga, 1978.
Chastelet, Jacques, *La vie quotidienne en Espagne au temps de Goya*, Paris, 1966.
Clonard, Conde de, *Historia Organica de la Infanteria y Caballeria Española*, 16 Vols., Madrid, 1847–1856, Vols. 5 and 6.
Clonard, Conde de, *Album de la Caballeria Española*, Madrid, 1861.
Clonard, Conde de, *Album de la Infanteria Española*, Madrid, 1861.
Estado Militar de España, Madrid, 1800, 1808.
Estudio Historico del Cuerpo de Ingeniero del Ejercito, 2 Vols., Madrid, 1911, Vol. 2.
Herrero Fernandez-Quesada, Maria Dolores, *La ense*, Segovia, 1990.
Hugo, A., *France Militaire*, 5 Vols., Paris, 1833–1838, Vol. 1 to 3.
Larriategui, Felix colon de, *Compendio de las Juzgados Militares*, 2 Vols., Madrid, 1793.
Medina Avila, Carlos J., *Organizacion y Uniformes de la Artilleria Española*, Madrid, 1992.
Pivka, Otto von, *Spanish Armies of the Peninsular War*, Osprey, London, 1975.
Vigon Suero-Diaz, Jorge, *Historia de la Artilleria Española*, 3 Vols., Madrid, 1947, Vol. 2.

Navy Brigadier Dionisio Alcala Galiano, c. 1800. Galiano was a distinguished officer who made important explorations on the north-west coast of America with Malaspina. He was killed at Trafalgar. He wears a dark blue coat with scarlet cuffs, collar and turnbacks, gold buttons and gold lace edging the facings. In this case, the gold lace also edges the bottom of the coat. The three gold laces with a silver twisted lace indicate the brigadier's rank. (Museo Naval, Madrid)

THE PLATES

PLATE A: CAMPAIGNS AGAINST THE FRENCH, 1793–95

A1: Chasseur, La Reine Émigré Legion Formed in early 1793 by order of Gen. Ricardos, the legion bore several names and initially had a squadron of hussars which were dismounted and served as foot soldiers. They were finally disbanded in about June 1794, leaving a corps of about 1,200 men divided into six companies including one of chasseurs and one of grenadiers. The legion fought in many engagements during the Roussillon campaign and it is interesting to note that Gen. La Union, for instance, took care to have them evacuated if there was any danger of their imprisonment; for émigrés, death by French republican firing squads was a certainty. As a result, there are accounts of isolated parties of émigrés fighting to the death rather than surrender. In May 1795, the legion was transferred to Cadiz, then moved to Zamora where it was incorporated into the Borbon Regiment in January 1796. The chasseur's uniform was white with scarlet facings, pewter buttons and a round hat whose white-edged brim was turned up on the left side with a green plume. (Grouvel, Baron de, *Les Troupes de l'Émigration Française*, 3 Vols., Paris, 1958, Vol. 3; De Franclieu, 'Souvenirs de l'Émigration en Espagne', *La Sabretache*, February 1931)

A2: Fusilier, Africa Regiment This innovative brown campaign dress was introduced from 1793 for troops fighting the French in the Pyrenees. We cannot be absolutely certain that the Africa Regiment wore it, but as this unit served during the whole campaign from 1793 to 1795, the chances are fairly good. The uniform would have been trimmed with the black regimental facings.

On 30 July 1795, two battalions of the regiment posted at the Ollareguy Pass managed to hold off a superior French force by firing an opening volley and charging the French column at bayonet point. Col. Goyeneta was killed in the ensuing hand-to-hand fighting, but the French attack was compromised. Moved by such valour, the king allowed an honour badge to be worn by the 1st and 2nd battalions on their sleeves.

A3: Trooper, Algarbe Cavalry Regiment Algarbe was one of several cavalry regiments which took part in the Roussillon campaign in 1793–1794. It mustered 457 men in early 1794. The scarlet and yellow dress of the regiment was colourful, but its cut was typical of Spanish cavalry units until 1796, when many changes were made.

PLATE B: DEFENCE OF CADIZ AGAINST THE BRITISH, 1797

B1: Sergeant, Marine Artillery Brigades A third of the brigades were based in Cadiz where there was also a naval Royal Academy of Artillery. During the British attack of 5–7 July 1797, some of the marine gunners manned floating batteries. The marine artillery wore blue faced with scarlet, and from 1795, had black gaiters and plain hats. It also had its own system for showing the ranks of NCOs and gunners on the coat cuffs. The gold lace edging the cuff and its buttonholes denoted the rank of *Primer Condestable*, a senior sergeant.

B2: Fusilier, Cordoba Regiment Cordoba was one of several infantry regiments that participated in the defence of Cadiz. It had a white uniform with scarlet facings, violet collars, brass buttons. Hats probably still had the yellow tape binding at the time of the British attack.

B3: Officer, Cadiz Urban Militia The urban militia of the port city of Cadiz was organised into 20 companies of 100 men, and participated in the defence of the city during the British attack. From 1762 and into the early 1790s, its uniform was blue with white waistcoats and cuffs, black collars, gold buttons and gold lace edging the coat and waistcoat. The collar was changed to white, and gold-edged white lapels were added, probably in the mid-1790s. (José Bueno, *Andalucia y sus Milicias*, Malaga, 1990)

PLATE C: DEFENCE OF TENERIFE AGAINST THE BRITISH, 1797

C1: Fusilier, Canarias Battalion When Commodore Nelson's squadron attacked Santa Cruz in late July 1797, most of the Spanish regulars belonged to this battalion, which was raised on 31 December 1792 and formed during 1793. When Nelson attacked, it had 247 men at Santa Cruz. Its first uniform was white with scarlet collars, cuffs and piping, pewter buttons, and hats edged with white lace. Green lapels piped scarlet were added probably not too long afterwards and it is assumed they had them by 1797.

C2: Fusilier, Canarias Militia Various corps of militia in the port of Santa Cruz and nearby locations on the island of Tenerife were mobilised and served bravely against the British attackers. Their uniform was blue faced with scarlet. (Sketch of a *c.*1797 militiaman, Museo Militar Regional de Canarias)

Marine Artillery gunner, 1789, wearing a blue coat with blue turnbacks and breeches, red collar, cuffs and lapels, brass buttons, and yellow hat lace. The wooden mortar bed is painted red. (Anne S.K. Brown Military Collection, Brown University, Providence. Ph: R. Chartrand)

LEFT **Marine Infantry fusilier, c. 1801.** Blue coat with blue collar and turnbacks, red cuffs, brass buttons, and yellow hat lace. (Anne S.K. Brown Military Collection, Brown University, Providence. Ph: R. Chartrand)

RIGHT **Marine Infantry grenadier, 1789.** From 1789 there were 19 grenadiers in each company of marines. Their cuffs were to have a yellow grenade badge and a thin yellow edging. They wore blue uniforms with red cuffs, brass buttons, white turnbacks, and grenadier bearskin caps. (Anne S.K. Brown Military Collection, Brown University, Providence. Ph: R. Chartrand)

C3: Gunner, Real Artilleria Regiment The artillery at Santa Cruz which devastated the British attackers was served by a mixed force of regular gunners assisted by militia artillerymen. The regular gunners had the blue uniform shown; the militiamen probably had the same with scarlet lapels.

PLATE D: 'WAR OF THE ORANGES', PORTUGAL, 1801

D1: Fusilier, Yann (Swiss) Regiment Swiss regiments on Spanish pay wore blue coats. They were raised by 'capitulation', or contract with Swiss colonels whose regiment bore their names, but although the regiment's title could often change, the Swiss units were always up to the established strength laid down by the Spanish government. Col. Yann's 1793 capitulation specified a total of 1,907 officers and men divided into two battalions, each having a company of grenadiers and four of fusiliers.

D2: Fusilier, Navarra Regiment This regiment was one of the many deployed by Spain against Portugal. The white uniform was typical of Spain's infantry during this conflict. Navarra wore sky blue and scarlet facings, and the piping is also often shown edging the waistcoat as well. (1801 uniform plates, A.S.K. Brown Military Collection)

D3: Trooper, Guardia de Corps, American Company The Life Guards were among the first to have the lapels squared and closed down to the waist. The 'American' company was composed of young men from wealthy and noble colonial families from Spanish America. Its bandoleer was violet.

PLATE E: THE 1802 UNIFORMS

E1: Officer, Infantry After nearly a hundred years of wearing white uniforms with various regimental colours, the whole line infantry was assigned sky blue with black facings piped red. While the men now had coatees with squared, closed lapels at the waist, officers had long-tailed coats with scarlet turnbacks. In theory, their lapels were to be as the men's, but some obviously preferred the cut-away style as shown on this figure, which is based on a portrait of a young officer by José Campeche in the Museo Historico Municipal, Cadiz.

E2: Private, Light Infantry Light infantry units which had hitherto worn a variety of uniforms often based on Spanish regional costumes were now ordered into a Hungarian hussar-style green uniform with scarlet facings and yellow cords, the headgear vaguely resembling the British Tarleton helmet.

E3: Trooper, Mounted Chasseurs All regiments were assigned an emerald green hussar-style uniform with scarlet collars and cuffs with white cords. They were also supposed to wear the Tarleton helmet, but shakos were obviously worn by units in Denmark during 1807, according to Suhr's plates.

PLATE F: MARINES AT TRAFALGAR, 1805

F1: Private, Marine Infantry Brigade From 1802, the marine infantrymen had a blue coatee with scarlet collar, cuffs, lapels and turnbacks, brass buttons and an anchor at the collar. Marines continued to wear the cut-away lapels for a few years. Only in 1807 are the closed, squared lapels shown. (Museo Naval, Madrid, c. 1802–1805 uniform watercolours; José Maria Bueno, *La Infanteria y la Artilleria de Marina 1537–1931*, Malaga, 1985)

F2: Corporal, Marine Infantry Brigade, undress The marines had a shipboard undress uniform of brown and red. An order of January 1805 mentioned brown ponchos, jackets and trousers, scarlet collars, small lapels and piping for the jacket, brass anchors for the jacket's collar, scarlet piping for trousers, and fatigue caps with scarlet turn-ups. (Museo Naval, Madrid, Ms 1375)

F3: Gunner, Marine Artillery From 1802, the naval artilleryman's uniform had blue lapels but kept the long scarlet turnbacks. Sergeants now had gold and crimson silk epaulettes, ordered to be of crimson silk only on 24 October 1805. (Museo Naval, Madrid, Ms 1375 & 2311)

PLATE G: THE 1805 UNIFORMS

G1: Fusilier, 1st Barcelona Light Infantry The light infantry completely changed its uniform style yet again in 1805, swapping the green hussar dress for a blue uniform which was much closer to standard military fashions. Each regiment had different facings. The head-dress was to be a bicorn with a green plume, but units sent with Romana to Denmark had shakos.

G2: Officer, Maria Luisa Hussars This figure is based on a full-length portrait painted in 1808 by Francisco Goya of Capt. Pantaleon Perez de Nenin. Spanish hussars had pelisses with tall collars of the facing colour, and company officers put their epaulettes on as well, distinctions not seen in most other armies.

G3: Grenadier, Principe Infantry Regiment This regiment, one of the oldest in the Spanish army, wore white faced with violet. Spanish grenadiers still wore the very tall fur cap with the long and richly embroidered bag. Their cuffs had laces in the button colour. On the accoutrements were hangers, as well as a brass match case, a traditional rather than a useful item. Principe was deployed in Portugal in 1807 but joined the fight against the French the following year.

PLATE H: BATTLE OF BAILEN, 1808

H1: Fusilier, Tercios de Texas The two *tercios* amounted to one battalion of 436 officers and men, and was part of Lt. Gen. Teodoro Reding's 1st Division which was most heavily engaged in the battle. Its uniform was blue faced with scarlet and edged with yellow lace.

H2: Officer, Provincial Militia The provincial militia battalions of Granada, Trujillo, Bujalance, Cuenca and Ciudad Real, all part of Mariscal de Campo Marquis Coupigny's 2nd Division, were in action. All provincial militia battalions had the same uniform of white faced with scarlet. ('La Batalla de Bailen', *Researching & Dragona*, Enero 1997)

H3: Trooper, Numancia Dragoon Regiment One squadron of 140 men, all mounted, of this unit was with Reding's 1st Division which fought at Bailen. The uniform was yellow faced with black and trimmed with white lace. (E. Gavira y Perez de Varga and S. Marcos Rodriguez, *El Regimiento Numancia en la Historia de España*, c. 1992)

Navy Administration officer, c. 1805–10, wearing a blue coat and breeches, scarlet collar, cuffs, lining and waistcoat, gold buttons and lace. Army Administration officers had the same uniform, but with silver buttons and lace. Painting by J.B. Vernay. (Museo Nacional de Cuba, Havana)

Notes sur les planches en couleur

A1 Chasseur, Émigré de La Reine. Légion. Son uniforme est blanc aux parements écarlates, avec des boutons en étain et un chapeau rond bordé de blanc, dont le bord était relevé du côté gauche par un plumet vert. **A2** Fusilier, Régiment d'Afrique. Cet uniforme de campagne novateur, de couleur marron, fut introduit à partir de 1793 pour les troupes qui se battaient avec les Français dans les Pyrénées. Cet uniforme aurait été orné de parements régimentaires noirs. **A3** Soldat de cavalerie, régiment de cavalerie d'Algarbe. L'uniforme écarlate et jaune de ce régiment était original, mais sa coupe était typique de la cavalerie espagnole jusqu'en 1796. A cette date, on introduisit beaucoup de changements.

B1 Sergent, Brigades d'artillerie marines. L'artillerie marine portait des uniformes bleus aux parements écarlates et, à partir de 1795, des guêtres noires et un chapeau tout simple. Le rang des sous-officiers et des canonniers apparaissait sur les revers des manches de la capote. Le galon doré qui borde la manchette et ses boutonnières dénote un Primer Condestable ou sergent-chef. **B2** Fusilier, Régiment de Cordoue, qui porte un uniforme blanc aux parements écarlates, col violet, boutons en cuivre. Les chapeaux portaient sans doute toujours la fixation à ganse jaune à l'époque de l'attaque britannique. **B3** Officier, milice urbaine de Cadiz. A partir de 1762 et jusqu'à 1790, cet uniforme était bleu, avec un gilet et des poignets blancs, un col noir, des boutons dorés et un galon doré qui bordait la capote et le gilet. Le col devint blanc et on ajouta des revers bordés d'un galon doré, sans doute vers 1795.

C1 Fusilier, Bataillon de Canarias. Le premier uniforme de ce bataillon était blanc avec un col, des poignets et un passepoil écarlates, des boutons en étain et un chapeau bordé de galon blanc. Des revers verts passepoilés d'écarlate furent sans doute ajoutés peu après et on pense qu'ils existaient en 1797. **C2** Fusilier, Milice de Canarias. Leur uniforme était bleu aux parements écarlates. **C3** Canonnier, Régiment d'artillerie de Real. Les canonniers réguliers portaient l'uniforme bleu illustré ici, et les miliciens avaient sans doute le même, avec des revers écarlates.

D1 Fusilier, Régiment d'Yann (Suisse). Les régiments suisses engagés par l'Espagne portaient une capote bleue. **D2** Fusilier, Régiment de Navarre. Ils portaient un uniforme bleu ciel aux parements écarlates. Le passepoil apparaît souvent sur le gilet également. (planches d'uniformes 1801, Collection militaire A.S.K. Brown) **D3** Soldat de cavalerie, Guardia de Corps, Compagnie américaine. Les gardes royaux furent parmi les premiers à porter des revers carrés et fermés jusqu'à la taille. La bandoulière était violette.

E1 Officier d'infanterie. En 1802, toute l'infanterie reçut des uniformes bleu ciel aux parements noirs bordés de rouge. Les hommes avaient une veste aux revers carrés et fermés à la taille alors que les officiers avaient une veste à queue-de-pie aux revers écarlates. Leurs revers devaient être les mêmes que ceux des soldats, mais certains préféraient le style dégagé, comme le montre cette figure. **E2** Simple soldat, infanterie légère. Les unités d'infanterie légère reçurent l'ordre de porter un uniforme vert hongrois de style hussard, avec des parements écarlates et des cordons jaunes. **E3** Soldat de cavalerie, Chasseurs à cheval. Tous les régiments reçurent un uniforme vert émeraude de style hussard, avec un col et des manchettes écarlates ornées de cordons blancs. Ils étaient aussi censés porter le casque Tarleton, mais il est évident que les unités au Danemark portaient le shako.

F1 Simple soldat, brigade d'infanterie marine. A partir de 1802, les soldats d'infanterie de marine portaient une veste bleue avec un col, des manchettes et des revers écarlates, des boutons en cuivre et une ancre sur le col. Les fusiliers marins continuèrent à porter les revers de jaquette pendant plusieurs années. **F2** Caporal, brigade d'infanterie marine, petite tenue. Les fusiliers marins avaient une petite tenue de marron et rouge qu'ils portaient à bord. **F3** Simple soldat, artillerie marine. A partir de 1802, l'uniforme du soldat d'artillerie comportait les revers bleus mais conservait les longs retours écarlates. Les sergents portaient maintenant des épaulettes dorées et cramoisies en soie, qui furent modifiées le 24 octobre 1805 pour devenir cramoisies seulement.

G1 Fusilier, 1er régiment d'infanterie légère de Barcelone. L'infanterie légère modifia totalement son uniforme encore une fois en 1805, abandonnant l'uniforme hussard vert en faveur d'un uniforme bleu. Chaque régiment avait des parements différents. Le couvre-chef était un bicorne orné d'un plumet vert, mais les unités envoyés avec La Romana au Danemark portaient le shako. **G2** Officier, Hussards de Maria Luisa. Les hussards espagnols portaient une pelisse à col haut de la couleur des parements, et les officiers de compagnie portaient aussi leurs épaulettes. **G3** Grenadier, Régiment d'infanterie de Principe. Ce régiment portait un uniforme blanc aux parements violets. Les grenadiers espagnols portaient toujours le très grand bonnet à poil et le long sac richement brodé. Leurs manchettes portaient du galon de la même couleur que les boutons. Sur le matériel se trouvaient des crochets, ainsi qu'une boîte à allumettes en cuivre.

H1 Fusilier, Tercios de Texas. L'uniforme était bleu aux parements écarlates et bordé de galon jaune. **H2** Officier, Milice provinciale. Tous les bataillons de milice provinciale avaient le même uniforme blanc aux parements violets. **H3** Soldat de cavalerie, régiment de dragons de Numancia. Cet uniforme était jaune aux parements noirs, orné de galon blanc.

Farbtafeln

A1 Chasseur, La Reine Emigré-Legion. Die Uniform dieses Soldaten ist weiß mit scharlachroten Aufschlägen und Zinnknöpfen. Der runde Hut weist eine weiß-eingefaßte Krempe auf, die auf der linken Seite mit einem grünen Federbusch aufgesteckt ist. **A2** Füsilier, Afrika-Regiment. Diese neuartige braune Felduniform wurde ab 1793 bei den Truppen eingeführt, die in den Pyrenäen gegen die Franzosen kämpften. Es ist anzunehmen, daß die Uniform mit den schwarzen Regimentsaufschlägen versehen war. **A3** Einfacher Soldat, Algarbe-Kavallerieregiment. Die scharlachrote und gelbe Uniform des Regiments war zwar bunt, aber der Schnitt war bis 1796 typisch für die spanischen Kavallerie-Einheiten. Danach wurden zahlreiche Veränderungen vorgenommen.

B1 Feldwebel, Marineartillerie-Brigaden. Die Marineartillerie trug blaue Uniformen mit scharlachroten Aufschlägen und ab 1795 schwarze Gamaschen und einfarbige Hüte. Der Rang eines Unteroffiziers oder eines Schützen war an den Jackenmanschetten zu erkennen. Die Einfassung der Manschetten und des Knopfloches mit Goldlitze bezeichnete einen Primer Condestable, also einen Oberfeldwebel. **B2** Füsilier, Cordoba-Regiment. Der Soldat trägt eine weiße Uniform mit scharlachroten Aufschlägen, violettem Kragen und Messingknöpfen. Zur Zeit des britischen Angriffs hatten die Hüte wahrscheinlich noch das gelbe Band. **B3** Offizier, städtische Bürgerwehr von Cadiz. Ab 1762 bis Anfang der 90er Jahre des 18. Jahrhunderts war die Uniform der Bürgerwehr blau mit weißen Westen und Manschetten, schwarzem Kragen, Goldknöpfen und Goldlitzeneinfassung an der Jacke und der Weste. Die Farbe des Kragens wechselte zu weiß, und vermutlich Mitte der 90er Jahre des 18. Jahrhunderts wurden goldfarben eingefaßte, weiße Revers hinzugefügt.

C1 Füsilier, Canarias-Bataillon. Die erste Uniform dieses Bataillons war weiß mit scharlachroten Kragenspiegeln, Manschetten und Vorstößen und hatte Zinnknöpfe. Die Hüte waren mit weißer Litze eingefaßt. Die grünen Revers mit scharlachroter Einfassung kamen wahrscheinlich schon bald danach auf, und es ist anzunehmen, daß sie 1797 bereits in Umlauf waren. **C2** Füsilier, Canarias-Miliz. Die Uniform der Miliz war blau mit scharlachroten Aufschlägen. **C3** Schütze, Real Artillerie-Regiment. Die regulären Schützen trugen die abgebildete blaue Uniform, die Milizionäre trugen wahrscheinlich die gleiche Uniform mit scharlachroten Revers.

D1 Füsilier, Yann (schweizerisches) Regiment. Schweizerische Regimenter im spanischen Dienst trugen blaue Waffenröcke. **D2** Füsilier, Navarra-Regiment. Die Soldaten des Navarra-Regiments trugen eine himmelblaue Uniform mit scharlachroten Aufschlägen. Häufig sieht man die Vorstöße auch als Einfassung auf der Weste. (Farbtafeln der Uniformen von 1801, A.S.K. Brown Military Collection) **D3** Einfacher Soldat, Guardia de Corps, Amerikanische Kompanie. Die Soldaten der Leibgarde gehörten zu den ersten Uniformträgern mit eckigen, geschlossenen Aufschlägen in Taillenhöhe. Das Bandolier war violett.

E1 Offizier, Infanterie. 1802 erhielt die gesamte Linieninfanterie himmelblaue Uniformen mit rot eingefaßten, schwarzen Aufschlägen. Während die Mannschaftsgrade einen enganliegenden, kurzen Waffenrock mit eckigen, geschlossenen Aufschlägen in Taillenhöhe trugen, hatten die Offiziere Jacken mit langen Schößen und scharlachroten Aufschlägen. Eigentlich sollten ihre Aufschläge denen der Mannschaften gleichen, doch zogen manche Offiziere offensichtlich die angeschnittene Form vor, wie man an dieser Abbildung sieht. **E2** Gefreiter, leichte Infanterie. Die Einheiten der leichten Infanterie hatten sich nun laut Befehl in einer grünen Uniform im ungarischen Husarenstil zu kleiden, die scharlachrote Aufschläge und gelbe Tressen aufwies. **E3** Einfacher Soldat, berittene Chasseurs. Alle Regimenter erhielten eine smaragdgrüne Uniform im Husarenstil. Sie hatte scharlachrote Kragenspiegel und Manschetten sowie weiße Tressen. Außerdem verlangte die Vorschrift eigentlich das Tragen des Tarleton-Helms, doch trugen die Einheiten in Dänemark offensichtlich Tschakos.

F1 Gefreiter, Marineinfanterie-Brigade. Ab 1802 trugen die Marineinfanteristen einen blauen, enganliegenden, kurzen Waffenrock. Die Kragen, die Manschetten, Revers und Aufschläge waren scharlachrot. Die Jacke hatte Messingknöpfe und wies am Kragen einen Anker auf. Die Marineinfanteristen trugen die angeschnittenen Revers noch ein paar Jahre lang. **F2** Obergefreiter, Marineinfanterie-Brigade, Interimsuniform. Die Marineinfanteristen hatten eine braun-rote Interimsuniform für an Bord. **F3** Gefreiter, Marineartillerie. Ab 1802 hatte die Uniform der Marineartillerie blaue Revers, doch wurden die langen, scharlachroten Aufschläge beibehalten. Feldwebel hatten damals goldfarbene und purpurrote Seidenepauletten. Die Vorschrift, ausschließlich purpurrote Seidenepauletten zu tragen, erging erst am 24. Oktober 1805.

G1 Füsilier, 1. Barcelona Leichte Infanterie. Die leichte Infanterie änderte 1805 erneut ihren Uniformstil von Grund auf. An die Stelle der grünen Husarenuniform trat eine blaue Uniform. Jedes Regiment hatte unterschiedliche Uniformaufschläge. Die Kopfbedeckung war ein Zweispitz mit einem grünen Federbusch, allerdings trugen die Einheiten, die mit La Romana nach Dänemark geschickt wurden, Tschakos. **G2** Offizier, Maria Luisa-Husaren. Die spanischen Husaren trugen Umhänge mit hohen Stehkrägen in der Aufschlagsfarbe. Kompanieoffiziere trugen außerdem noch ihre Epauletten. **G3** Grenadier, Principe-Infanterieregiment. Dieses Regiment trug eine weiße Uniform mit violetten Aufschlägen. Spanische Grenadiere trugen damals noch die sehr hohe Pelzmütze mit dem langen, reich verzierten Kopfteil. Die Manschetten wiesen Litzen in der Farbe der Knöpfe auf. Am Zubehör befanden sich Aufhänger und eine Streichholzschachtel aus Messing.

H1 Füsilier, Tercios de Texas. Die Uniform war blau und hatte scharlachrote Aufschläge. Sie war mit gelber Litze eingefaßt. **H2** Offizier, Provinz-Miliz. Alle Bataillone der Provinz-Miliz hatten die gleiche weiße Uniform mit scharlachroten Aufschlägen. **H3** Einfacher Soldat, Numancia Dragoner-Regiment. Die Uniform war gelb mit schwarzen Aufschlägen. Sie war mit weißer Litze eingefaßt.